Praise for **UTTER, EARTH**

"*Utter, Earth* leaps, ranges, delves—or should I say rabbits, antelopes, and elephant seals? Isaac Yuen's playful, precise book will delight biologist and linguaphile alike. With persnickety glee and accuracy, he holds obscure facts of the more-than-human world up to the light in a style that's a mashup of Rachel Carson, Gary Larson, Ross Gay, David Sedaris, and David Attenborough. The enthusiasm and delight of *Utter, Earth* is infectious, and that's just the point. Yuen wants us to fall in love with the beings we share this amazing planet with, to realize the human way of living, breathing, birthing, eating, working, and caring is not the acme but just one option among many wonderful, amazing ways of being—and we could perhaps learn a thing or two from dung beetles and hagfish if we allowed ourselves to be curious. I laughed aloud while reading *Utter, Earth*, and the naturalist in me bows to the huge body of knowledge and research that permits Yuen's accuracy to sing with such a light touch. Do yourself a favor and read every page, including the 'Brief Thoughts on Almost Every Mentioned, Mostly Living Thing' that serves as a quasi-appendix. You'll leave your chair ready to appreciate the world around you anew."

—Elizabeth Bradfield, naturalist, author of *Toward Antarctica*, and coeditor of *Cascadia Field Guide: Art, Ecology, Poetry*

"To shoal is to be social, to sense together, we learn in one of Yuen's more-than-human essays. But to school is to sweep together in unison, to dazzle wi
schooling that animates *Utter, E*

T0286021

curiosity, play, and care—aim to weave us back into a world of which we are but one small part. How would our language change if we invited nonhuman others alongside us again in fellowship, if our lives not only allowed for but celebrated everything swimming just beyond the limits of what we know? It's not time for school, it's time to school, to school with the creatures of *Utter, Earth*, the lemurs, leopards, and leafcutter ants, the wombats, waterbuck, and wildebeest, to school with others to find ourselves again."

—David Naimon, host of *Between the Covers*

"In *Utter, Earth*, animals and language are alive: rollicking, wild, enthralling. Isaac Yuen writes with so much enchantment and humour, this is a book that will upend how you see the natural world—and our own place in it."

—Jessica J. Lee, author of *Two Trees Make a Forest* and *Dispersals*

Utter, Earth

Advice on Living in a More-than-Human World

Isaac Yuen

WEST VIRGINIA UNIVERSITY PRESS
MORGANTOWN

ISBN 978-1-959000-15-0 (paperback) / 978-1-959000-16-7 (ebook)

Library of Congress Control Number: 2023043227

Cover design and images by Julian Montague
Book design by Than Saffel / WVU Press

A version of "The Perfect Party Guest" first appeared as "Giving Up on Your
Dreams" in a publication of the Center for Humans and Nature Press on
February 1, 2023, and is revised and reprinted here with permission of the Center
for Humans and Nature Press.

AKADEMIE DER KÜNSTE

Supported by the Akademie der Künste, Berlin, with funding from the Federal
Government Commissioner for Culture and the Media as part of the NEUSTART
KULTUR programme.

To Michaela, one who converses with forests,
both urging me to aim higher

A LITTLE madness in the Spring
Is wholesome even for the King,
But God be with the Clown,
Who ponders this tremendous scene–
This whole experiment of green,
As if it were his own!

—*Emily Dickinson*

Contents

List of Illustrations

1. Din

Weddell seals vocalize nine types of sounds beyond the range of human hearing. Guinea baboons learn to grunt in the accent of their preferred social group. Glass frogs pitch their calls higher near roaring waterfalls while waving hello to potential mates. The croaks of male Gulf corvina resemble underwater machine-gun fire in sound and decibel level; spawning aggregations can induce hearing loss in nearby marine mammals. Deaf, earless moths sport wing scales that dampen predatory sonar. Bats can crash into sponge walls that produce weak echoes, not unlike people walking into glass doors. Solitary minke whales seem to abandon efforts to hear and be heard in waters with heavy shipping and military activities. The album *Songs of the Humpback Whale* officially reached interstellar space in August 2012 onboard *Voyager 1*; it is not part of the Golden Record's "Sounds of Earth" track with tame dogs, wild dogs, and hyenas but mixed in among the recorded human "Hellos" in fifty-five languages. In approximately forty thousand years, the probe will drift within 1.6 light-years of Gliese 445, a star in the constellation of Camelopardalis. What we think of as a giraffe is in reality four genetically distinct species—some of which have been recorded humming at night. Researchers are unsure if these sounds are passive, like snores, or active messages intended for fellow giraffes, swaying in the dark.

Yes, You Can Leave the Hospital Without Naming Your Baby

up to two weeks before having to file the birth certificate paperwork; unless you live in Germany, where you have up to three months to find a moniker for the soon-to-be toddler before the state decides on your behalf. Or so I've been told. Regardless, it is wise to take the time to choose carefully, for some newborns can be one way in the womb and another out in the world. The Emma highlighted from the big book of names may not match the Bernadette you now cradle in your arms. Please forgive their tiny change of hearts. It is hard to hear clearly through a bellyful of fluid, so while they might have cooed at Liam while contained, they may bawl up a storm after discharge, unless you can conjure up distractions like calling them Li-HAAM, of which the yelling of the second half might usher in a fit of giggly delight, and then lead to permutations of Hammy, or Hamster, or even Sir Ham-Ham of Hamalot. Or so I've heard.

*

Of course, you can simply impose your will upon another, stamp your hopes and dreams onto any newly minted thing. This is the easiest and most unfair way to establish a relationship. Celebrities with their outsized egos do this on the regular, turning their hapless offspring into benign fruit, like Apple, or branding that means everything and nothing, like Goop. Ex-power couples may choose to dedicate their progeny to ex-prototype spy planes (preceded by Æ, which, according to the former

Musks, is the "elvish rendition of artificial intelligence") or to syllables of the Semitic abjads (here, at least Aleph Portman-Millepied has decent nickname potential, like Al or Alf or Alfonso Soriano and maybe even the Fonz, but rare is any child suave enough to pull off the latter sobriquet).

*

In the wild reaches, even less care is taken in the naming process. This is understandable, given that there are so many mushrooms and so many weevils, and everything adjacent to groups or branching from clades merits a station within life's grand catalog. Overworked taxonomists may be too mossy-brained to conjure up yet more original labels after being tasked to come up with 1.3 million of them, often in both common and Latin scientific. Under such pressure some have resorted to the celebrity method but in reverse, so that the world is now blessed with the beauty of the Kate Winslet beetle, which may never sink beneath the waves but may yet still go under if its Costa Rican treetops are converted to pasture. Then there is the Bono's Joshua Tree trapdoor spider, who has likely never heard its U2 counterpart sing but definitely scuttles beneath the desert national park, where the unpaved streets go unnamed.

*

When mired in designation indecision, one solution is to resort to using luminaries past or present: Darwin or Attenborough are fashionable go-tos these days. One could also pay tribute to the venerated yet underrated Friedrich Wilhelm Heinrich Alexander von Humboldt. It is hard to tell whether the nineteenth-century Prussian polymath would derive pleasure from having so many things under the sun named after him, a list that includes not only white-throated penguins and hog-nosed skunks but also a productive oceanic current, an entire region on the moon, and a pair of asteroids slinging around space why not. Without knowing the naturalist personally, it is difficult to gauge whether Humboldt would be humbled by such label-mad adulation or exasperated at the lack of imagination used to convey the splendors he saw all around, so succinctly captured in the dying words of his similarly multinamed brother, Friedrich Wilhelm Christian Karl Ferdinand von Humboldt, the genius linguist of the family: *Wie großartig diese Strahlen! Sie scheinen die Erde zum Himmel zu winken!*

*

The main shame of nomenclature negligence is that it can lead to the careless assignment of value. Is the lesser kudu, with the same spiral horns shaped like Parmesan cheese straws, any less elegant and distinguished than its greater antelope cousin? Must the lesser frigatebird be relegated to notions of lower-class, second-rate, a notch-below, all the while soaring above the thermals with his red-throated kin bestowed with titles of "greater" and "magnificent"?

Of course there is the justification of size, which is usually a justification for laziness. The least weasel is not any less for weighing the same as a stack of pennies but should rather be lauded for its prowess in tackling prey ten times its size, severing the spines of baby bunnies with surgical bites. The least tern is not diminutive in any other aspect of its life, as the double-ounced ball of fluff is fully fit to embark on round-trip, fish-fueled flights from Nebraska to the Brazilian state of Ceará. (Here is not the last time where a nickname suits better than the proper title, as the oft-dubbed "little striker" reflects the bird's propensity to dive-bomb and defecate on anyone that encroaches upon its nest.) And of course we must thank the least bittern for being big enough to forgo any grudges that might arise from our naming slight, or so we assume its forbearance, not having heard any trace of bitterness in the cooing songs it sings through spring.

Sometimes being minuscule is what makes life possible in the first place, for being small may make you nontargetable to the many things that may otherwise wish to target you. Most foxes, if polled on their chicken-breed preferences, would rather avoid the hassle of defeathering a dozen Serama bantams when they could feast equivalently on one Jersey Giant. Mink farmers likely ran the numbers on the amount of weasel pelts needed for one fur coat before deciding to base their businesses on the larger family relation. Being Lilliputian in stature can also be advantageous should one find themselves residing on nonfictional Lilliputs, like the dwarf mammoths once did on Crete or the mini-mammoths once did on the Channel Islands of California, where compactness meant less time scrounging for food and more time enjoying ocean vistas. Yet any talk of reduced caloric intake would fall deaf on the North American least shrew, more commonly known as the North American horror show, at least to its subterranean neighbors. Driven by a heart revving at eight hundred beats a minute, the shrew avoids perishing by overexertion through practicing a regimen of overconsumption, devouring more than its body weight in food daily, caring not one whit whether that comes in the form of earthworms or sow bugs or the tails of unfortunate lizards trying to eke out a living, only to be forced to shed their precious appendages to appease the clockwork death machine. Should this shrew be deemed the least shrew, then all bears should be deemed least bears, for the shrew has no qualms about infiltrating beehives in the dead of winter to gorge on colonies too sluggish to defend themselves, biting off heads and crunching on thoraxes, leaving behind mangled wings and strewn abdomens for dismayed beekeepers, wayward in their belief that their charges would be safe behind electrified fences and the principles of hibernation.

*

But back to this GREATER, lesser, least business: Why the rabble-rousing around names, you say? What's in a silly title, you ask? It is the opinion of this observer that names are sacred things, and namings are sacred acts. Thus you can imagine their botheration toward the sort who, careless at best or malicious at worst, doles out names conflating dimensions with deficiencies, such as whoever christened the lesser earless lizard, or the lesser sooty owl, or the lesser mouse-deer. Gray souls most likely, rigid devotees to preserved specimens in amber jars or outdated treatises scribed on yellowed pages, working without much empathy in their hearts. Perhaps they do not realize that names might be all any of us have in the end, and that a few considerate details, a charitable word or two, might have afforded many a final fading easier to stomach and harder to forget, unlike what happened with the lesser mascarene flying foxes, which once congregated in tree hollows and became easy targets to smoke out and extinguish; or the Lesser Antillean rice rat from the Lesser Antilles chain of islands, so scarcely known and doubly diminished in reputation and geography that it winked out of existence without much ruckus. Then there was the case of the lesser bilby, a white-tailed, rabbit-eared bandicoot banished from the Australian outback back in the 1950s. Even its fierce and intractable spirit, so opposite of its gentler greater relative, could not endure without a physical vessel. The only concrete thing about the lesser bilby, besides the woefully nondescript name, is the constancy of its current status, as attested to in its official Northern Territory dossier, which contains this final line and epitaph: "No further conservation management plan can offer further help."

*

The next time you are tasked with naming a freshly forthed thing, do so with a measure of kindness. Resist the urge to name on a whim, for a good namer recognizes that naming can only be rightly done by knowing a life through its seasons, by sight and song, by fur or root. But don't fret overmuch on making mistakes. What is better than being a gifted namer is being an adaptable one, one willing to learn from past mistakes and able to make amends. This is a skill most paleontologists learn on the job, having to deal constantly with creatures so lacking in qualities most take for granted, such as being alive and being intact. We can learn much from those open-minded enough not to set names into stone, changing them when necessary to better fit the nature of their fossilized hosts, like when the *Brachiosaurus* displayed in Berlin was renamed a *Giraffatitan* from Tanzania, which was probably for the best, since most would agree that an African "titanic giraffe" hews closer to the truth than any European "arm lizard." Holding a flexible mindset can also help reflect a world striving to move beyond old egos and dusty traditions by drawing upon a richer reserve of culture and mythology, like the christening of *Hagryphus giganteus*, which melds the Egyptian god of the western desert with the ancient Greek's premixed lion-eagle, or *Ugrunaaluk kuukpikensis*, which means "Colville River's ancient grazer," not in distant Latin but in the living Alaskan Iñupiaq tongue that is still spoken in the area where the creature once dwelled so long ago.

*

Of course, better than being named by another is to discover a name for yourself, to attain that long-sought, hard-fought description that captures the essence of your being, the one that might not be so much spoken as made manifest. This is exemplified, for example, in the ancient branching gestures by what we call the bristlecone pine, or in the states of grace displayed by the entity some know simply as the peregrine. Once realized and embraced, this self-name cannot be co-opted by any outside powers, try as they might to hide it from sight, try as they will to erase it with official decrees or to slot it into classes below or beneath its deserved footing. To forge such a self demands a lot of soul-searching and practiced living, and the quest to attain it can be arduous. Sometimes the names we discover come to be single notes in a longer song, one that only reveals itself wholly at opportune moments, like when a lowly caterpillar emerges from its chrysalis as the Bhutan glory, or when a Diane's bare-hearted glass tadpole transforms into a Diane's bare-hearted glass frog, or the moment an Icelandic cyprine decides to trade in its drifting lifestyle to spend the next five centuries crafting its carbonate masterpiece one ring at a time. Perhaps

such a self-name is less of a set thing, less a flawless gem to be
hoarded in a safe, and more akin to breath, to water, as a process
in progress, fluid and ever-changing, part of the shimmer of a
sentence spoken while living life for life's sake, as something no
one, *no one*, can take away—this work, this dignity, this worth.

Second Best Is Best

Sometimes being at the top isn't all that it's cracked up to be, like if you were declared the world's tallest mountain one day by a Bengali mathematician and then named for a British surveyor you will never meet. The natural outcome of this is that tourists will start clambering over you, ascending your north and south sides, leaving tents and oxygen tanks and corpse after popsicled corpse on your slopes. No, sometimes it is better to trail a thousand feet below and cultivate your image cautiously, like how K2 worked its slow magic on Fosco Maraini over the years. "Just the bare bones of a name," the Italian mountaineer waxes about Earth's second highest peak, "all rock and ice and storm and abyss. It makes no attempt to sound human. It is atoms and stars. It has the nakedness of the world before the first man—Or of the cindered planet after the last." There's nothing quite like the feeling when someone takes the time to understand the persona you have tried so hard to project: in this case, rarefied and insuperable.

*

To be sure, there is not much rhyme or reason to how fame is attributed. What did the dinosaurs do to deserve their fanfare when the pseudosuchians were the first archosaurs to exercise terrestrial domination? Yet, no plushie line for the plate-covered aetosaurs. No book deal or feature films for *Saurosuchus*, T. Rex of the Triassic. And rare is the five-year-old who takes the time to pronounce *Dromicosuchus* over its five-syllabled dinosaur equivalent. But maybe in this case, the whole division is intentionally avoiding the limelight, preferring to lurk from the shadows to sport the last laugh, or at least one of those toothy grins that is the winning feature of many an alligator or crocodile, under-the-radar survivors that outlasted their rock-star relations. (Technically, birds are also dinosaurs, but I had not the heart to tell my local caiman—best to have them have this one small victory.)

*

Sometimes being best is the worst. The prized antlers the wapiti so lovingly nourishes with velvet and aspen shoots can turn their caretaker into rumpus room decor, even though deerstalkers know perfectly well they could just wait for the elk to finish bugling before picking up the discarded ornaments for a song. Then there is the case concerning the rhinoceros, where renown unsought steered many a soul to ruin. What a shame to almost unlock the formula for becoming a cult-hit success, being thick-skinned enough to shrug off predatory critique and humble enough to play second fiddle to the trunked giant everyone knows and loves. Unfortunately, the northern white rhinoceros in particular happened to feature the type of facial ornamentation that attracts the wrong type of attention. Who knew that a couple knobs of snout keratin could become such objects of desire for the poacher and such sources of sorrow for the poachee? Not long now until the answer becomes moot. Not long until Najin and Fatu, the last mother and daughter of the line, reunite with Sudan, past mate and former father, beyond the rim of this physical world.

*

Sometimes second best is good enough. The eastern brown snake may be runner-up to the inland taipan in venom strength, but it makes up for it in deadliness by being bad tempered and fleet of belly, which in this rare instance can be quicker than fleet of foot. And yes, one pepper contender may reign supreme in Scoville units when it comes to the Trinidad Moruga scorpion and the Komodo dragon varieties, but no sane person would care after tasting both, or remain sane for that matter, having to work through hours of numbness and general breathing difficulties post-ingestion. Sometimes attaining simply *a* high and not *the* high is all that matters, like if all you harbor is a craving for succulent squid. The sperm whale can attest to this compulsion, being perpetually ravenous for mantles and tentacles, plowing its brick of a head down a mile of ocean day in and day out to duel and devour creatures that spawned horror tales of old. Yet even this champion holder of innumerable records—largest toothed predator, loudest living creature (being able to hold its own in an argument with a rocket engine), most notorious albino literary nemesis—only snatches the bronze in the thing it tries its very best at, placing behind the smaller southern elephant seal and the Cuvier's beaked whale, both diving even deeper in their fanatical pursuit of choice cephalopod cuisine.

*

Accepting there will always be someone better may seem like failure to any perfectionist. How can you assess your worth without external metrics? What will you do instead of obsessing over usurpers of your records? After all, not everyone can be as gracious as the large-eared pika after the yellow-rumped leaf-eared mouse took its high-altitude crown, eking out a living four miles above sea level on the volcanic slopes of Llullaillaco between Argentina and Chile. Most of us less hardy folk would inevitably suffer some ego shock from this seeming demotion. The common swift, sleek and slick and regularly complimented, might have thought it was all that while cruising at seventy clicks until the Brazilian free-tailed bat came whipping through, all skin flap and finger bones and wrinkled lip, breaking a hundred without breaking a sweat. What is instructive here is that the swift knows to take this news in stride—or at least to take it in glide while swallowing dinner flies. In so doing, it has avoided the trap that has ensnared the cheetah, one who has molded life around its gold finish in the four-hundred-meter dash, so much so that it completely fails to qualify in all other categories of being a big cat, like being able to retract its claws or roar with authority like its lion and leopard cousins, both of whom regularly swing by to bully the cheetah out of its gazelle catches, at which the sprinting champ can only watch and pant, breathless and powerless.

*

Maybe the best thing about being the bridesmaid but never the bride is that you need never wed yourself wholly to any one thing. In this day and age of change and turmoil, it may be an advantage to be best at nothing but decent at many things. The panda bear and the koala bear and the monarch butterfly may grace the covers of boutique magazines dedicated to heirloom bamboo, gumleaf nutrition, and the art of finding the best milkweed plant for raising happy caterpillars, but it will be the raccoon and the coyote and the jellyfish, jimmying door handles and snatching up poodles and clogging power plant intakes, who will snag the leading roles in the Anthropocene. Such ne'er-do-wells won't garner any achievements of note for their performances except maybe the one that matters in the end, which is to prosper while living alongside a certain oblivious neighbor, one who is unaware of how much of a mess he has left behind, one ignorant in how he is using up more than his fair share, one so unchecked in appetite and obsessed with keeping up with the Joneses that he doesn't realize almost everyone in the neighborhood has long since moved away—including the Joneses—because who would want to live with such an over-bearing presence except those malleable enough to turn his vices into virtues, like the peppered moths of Manchester donning soot camouflage during the Industrial Revolution, or the crows of Sendai employing truck traffic to crack walnuts, or the white clovers of Norwegian farmlands tweaking their internal chemistries to thrive in hotter Indian cities? Some may deem them weeds and pests without much merit, but adaptability has always been too slippery an element to be quantified. Perhaps toward this end, it is better for us to eschew the notion of being best or even second best altogether, to see beyond achievements and acknowledge the beings behind them. This may entail that we seek out other ways of knowing altogether; less revolving around comparisons and record reverence and more embarking on trains of thought running on wonder and curiosity. When did the Madagascar tomato frog acquire its vine-ripened complexion? What prompts the springbok to "pronk" straight-legged, upward, again and again? How do whale barnacles secure prime humpback real estate amidst the vast and roiling seas? If anyone tries to dismiss these acts and their actors as silly or worthless, we shall laugh and agree that indeed they are so, and that we are also silly and worthless despite our best efforts to convince ourselves otherwise, being fortunate enough to live in a world that, despite our best efforts to improve upon it, remains chock-full of astonishment, so joyously inconsequential, so thoroughly indispensable.

2. Spectacle

Crucian carp can go temporarily blind while swimming through anoxic waters. Naked mole rats can survive eighteen minutes without oxygen by using a fructose-fed metabolic pathway normally associated with plants. Hummingbirds fuel their hovering by directly burning just-ingested nectar. The male *Calypte anna* orients his iridescent gorget opposite the sun to ensure females see an optimal hue of pink. Nocturnal dung beetles roll their dung in a straight path by the light of the Milky Way. Blind cave tetras possess left-bending skulls and swim counterclockwise in their lightless environment. Present-day hagfish have opaque patches over the places where their ancestors' eyes used to be. A squid's optic nerve routes behind its retina without interrupting the photoreceptor layer; thus, their eyes do not contain the blind spots vertebrate eyes have. Cuttlefish compensate for color blindness with wide, W-shaped pupils that maximize chromatic aberration, which distorts their vision such that they can access color information. The California two-spot octopus can sense changes in brightness through its skin without utilizing its central nervous system. Planarian flatworms exhibit negative phototaxis pre- and postdecapitation, suggesting a separate body-based reflex that responds to light. Vladimir Nabokov's 1945 musings that *Polyommatus* blue butterflies migrated to the New World across the Bering Strait was proven correct three decades after his death.

On Sights Unseen

Unlike Mr. E. R. Bradshaw of Napier Court (RIP), the pumpkin toadlet is quick to grasp the key lesson from the 1970 Monty Python film *How Not to Be Seen*, and that is to never heed the summons of British sketch comedians. The toadlet proves particularly resistant to being beckoned in general, possessing no eardrums with which to receive any kind of call, not even their own high-pitched chirps. (Why beckon when none among your kin can hear? Herpetologists are still pondering over this strange case of vestigial calling.) Frogs that are sound of hearing prove similarly weary to requests urging them to reveal themselves, probably gleaning from experience that disembodied narrators often manifest into full-bodied dangers, usually in forms of snakes or hawks or bird-eating spiders the size of small puppies. Tree frogs of the polka-dot variety have gone the extra mile toward not being seen, evolving biochemistry that renders their skin, bones, and even tissue fluids as leafy-hued as the surrounding canopy. One might think that having thus tamed the impulse of being enticed and having perfected impeccable disguises, tree frogs and their ilk are content to step behind the veil of this world like leprechauns, satisfied to dwell in myth and appear only in the occasional children's cereal commercial. But alas, tree frogs, like leprechauns, cannot help but crave to have their lucky charms and eat them too. Sometimes it is a delight to give your pursuers the slip, but sometimes it remains a thrill to let slip that glint of gold—it all depends on who is doing the chasing. Dyeing dart frogs balance attention seeking with attention averting by sporting inkblot patterns that are hard to mark out as "frog" when seen from afar but become blaring neon "FROG" for sore eyes up close. One moment, nothing but jungle thicket—another, a croaker impinging on your personal space! The abruptness of such manifestations can occasionally lead to awkward encounters, dividing parties into blunderers and the blundered into. This would be no bother if both entities were ardent, like frog and fellow frog suitor—*why, hello!*—or even if both were noncommittal, like frog and stray gooseberry—*smiley day to you!* But alas, the world is littered with complications even after rigorous filtration—see the aforementioned snakes and hawks and bird-eating spiders with legs the length of a child's forearm. Hence, dart frog poison exists to complement dart frog camouflage, combining to convey the following message: "Shoo, undesirables! Move along and nondisclose upon penalty of pain and cramping death!" While this is usually sufficient to deter most unwanted encounters, there remain some that cannot be avoided, like when dart frog meets pet parrot meets human versed in the art of tapirage, which involves said human catching said frog and plucking said parrot to rub its skin with frog poison, all in the hopes that the new feathers will grow back yellow with vermillion undertones. The ceremonial headdress fashioned from plumage produced in this way is very beautiful, but one cannot blame the frog for being resentful at becoming part of such a conspicuous artifact, which runs completely counter to its mandate of not being seen.

*

Sometimes, hiding in plain sight is indeed the soundest way to go unnoticed. Some accomplish this by being translucent and overclose, like eyelash mites clinging onto human faces. Others accomplish this by being bland and mass-produced, like yellow dent corn carpeting the Midwest. Forgettability can be attained by being too insignificant to be mulled over or by being too significant to be singled out. Yet there are those rare souls who can achieve both, like market apples at your local grocery. If you, like *Malus domestica*, can be everything to everyone—symbol to the religiously devout, paragon for the health-conscious, icon to tech giants and their late, fruit-loving founders—then the public may also welcome you without probing too deeply into your inner core. Be sweet enough or tart enough, be pie-worthy or cider-suited, and most will be too satisfied to discern that beneath your rosy exterior beats a gambler's heart, ready to drop it all to ride away on the whims of fate. Cut an upstanding Granny Smith along its equator and you will find a pentagram chamber, housing unruly seeds that will assuredly fall far from that first tree planted in the Sydney suburbs back in the 1860s, bearing fruit that will assuredly never again be named "best cooking apple of Australia." If indeed it is as Henry David Thoreau mused, that every wild apple shrub is a prince in disguise, then every apple seed contains a vagabond in return, ever eager to revert to its tramping ways. Once relieved of its people-pleasing pressures, apple seeds can tap into their genetic stores to reconfigure for a host of posthuman futures. One might lean on insights gained while thriving in Tasmania, where its Cleopatra-branded predecessor spent some time. Another may reach farther back, to France, whence its ancestors bore crabapples that made even the staunchest *pomme* connoisseur pucker. Still another might draw upon its ancient Kazakh lineage, back to the forerunner that operates presently under a wholly different guise: *Malus sieversii*, which remains to this day freer in form to be tree or shrub, wilder to tower tall or trail low, sometimes bewitching the bears of the nearby Tai Shan Mountains with fruit tasting of apricots, at others bearing crops so bitter as to be left alone, and so be beholden to no party save itself.

*

"'Tis a pity that apples cannot become spies." So might have lamented the intelligence community in their attempts to unearth talent as malleable as those in the *Malus* genus. Most likely, MI6 and the CIA have come to terms with the fact that non-plant-based plants must work harder to situate themselves into foreign environments. Contrary to pop culture depictions, the ideal undercover agent should not be suave or debonair, but rather nondescript in feature and thus easy to dismiss. The fourteen squirrels once accused of espionage by the Iranian government were likely not of the Indian giant variety, oversized rodents sporting lustrous coats of maroon and magenta, while Borneo tufted ground squirrels might be better suspects, as local legends have them deploying their fluffed tails as subterfuge against clouded leopards and slashing the throats of unsuspecting muntjac deer with their saw-ridge incisors. (No reports of such assassinations have been verified, which means that the squirrels were either entirely innocent or entirely masterful.) Most likely, the squirrel candidates in question were less showy than either, like the eastern grays of North America that have successfully invaded British and Italian forests, supplanting native populations and girdling commercial hardwood production. Still, it remains difficult to ascertain whether squirrels can become trained saboteurs without declassified documents, like there was for "Charlie" the robotic catfish, developed to collect enemy water in enemy rivers, or "Insectothopter," the dragonfly drone designed as a bug-carrying bug during the Cold War. Perhaps a squirrel's adorability is simply part of its cover, enhanced by a helter-skelter schtick that makes one question how it could ever carry out reconnaissance. To this day we only have one known case of infiltration by one Secret Squirrel™, albeit it takes the form of a Hanna-Barbara cartoon character equipped with a bulletproof coat, a cannon hat, and a machine-gun cane that goes *rata-tat-tat-tat!* "What an agent! What a squirrel!" What an earworm of a theme song!

*

There may come a day when you are picked out of a crowd despite your best efforts to lie low, like being selected for jury duty or being recruited to play your part in the human enterprise (which can include jury duty). Some candidates, like wild mustard and red jungle fowl, have embraced the latter request by embarking on the road toward domestication, transforming into broccolini and farmhouse poultry, respectively, becoming more heedable, herdable, and edible. Other borderline participants have pleaded their cases to be summarily dismissed from these ventures, like the cape buffalo, who is naturally gregarious and delicious but much too ill-tempered to be wrangled into pens or to listen long to testimony. The dreams of King Karl XI of Sweden to command a moose cavalry were shattered when these largest of deer grew frail in close quarters and panicky at the sound of musket fire. Lord Walter Rothschild may have paraded around

nineteenth-century London in his custom zebra-drawn carriage, but even he recognized their flighty, bitey, lion-anxious
natures, choosing instead to ride giant tortoises for fun instead.
Then there were times when fate itself seemed to interject
on behalf of the trajectory of a species, as it appeared to do
against the ambitions of US Congressman Robert Broussard,
who almost pushed through a bill in the late 1920s that would
have imported hippopotamuses to Louisiana as a domestic meat
source. We shall never know if Americans would have welcomed
"lake cow bacon" into their kitchens, but judging from the feral
hippos running rampant in Colombia after the death of their
keeper, drug kingpin Pablo Escobar, the animals may have
thrived in the bayous of the New World, munching on water
hyacinths, harassing airboat operators, and terrorizing native
alligators. Unlike tree frogs devising trick upon trick to remain
covert, or Sumatran rhinoceroses too shy and scarce to appear
even in essays about elusive creatures, hippopotamuses have no
problems hogging the spotlight, being boisterous, or indulging
in judicial processes, being seasoned (see *Community of Hippopotamuses Living in the Magdalena River v. Ministerio de Ambiente
y Desarrollo Sostenible et al.* [2021], in which hippos became
the first nonhuman animals to be recognized as "interested
persons" in US court history). Here is yet another direct, albeit
drastic way to be left to your own devices: lawyer up so that no
one will ever want to tangle with you again.

*

Maybe sometimes in life it pays to be hippo-like, badgering the
world into giving you your dues. But at other times, it might
be wise to be okapi-like, retreating inward to resemble your

understory surroundings. To know when to clamor and when to stifle—this lies in the realm of tactfulness, long practiced by singing toads and rustling oaks and yodeling loons, which are incidentally also dormant toads and placid oaks and reticent loons. Perhaps the glee of being seen by the world is always tempered by the fear of being betrayed by it, of being exploited by unscrupulous agents without consent or compensation. There is something to be said about being open to the bonds of kinship—the horse with her rider, the racer and his camel, the logging elephant and her mahout. Yet there is also something to be said about being wary of the perils of bondage—of spiked bits and saddle sores, of the rich's trafficking of child jockeys, of serving machinations that equate forests to processed board feet. How often do we *truly* heed the hearts of those we claim to tame and know, to see not through our eyes but rather theirs? How far are we able to venture outside our notions of utility or even beauty to truly perceive the other? Not often enough. Not far enough.

Yet there are instances, moments, when our species acts without regard for function or profit, and in so doing achieves some measure of redemption. Some of us brought *takhis* back to the Mongolian steppes because we could not bear that they had vanished, knowing fully these wild horses are nonrideable. Some of us work to protect the *havtagais* because we want them to continue to persist, knowing fully these wild camels will never yield. Most of us desire greatly to return elephant matriarchs to their ancestral lands, maybe driven by the knowledge that a few of us were the cause of their displacement. Despite or because of our collective crimes, our species can often be moved by a guilt we do not fully understand. Once, we drove the cave lion and the short-nosed bear and the Irish elk to their dooms. Once, we immortalized their spirits in charcoal and ochre inside caves of forgotten dreams. To this day, we raze and we tend. Even now, we maim and we weep. Perhaps burdened with the weight of what we have wrought, human beings have remained hauntable beings; and being hauntable means that we are still capable of turning our gaze, of looking up from our narrow preoccupations to be startled by the sight of a broader, vaster community. In so doing, we can come to realize a world that lies beyond us and use, and so come to see both the obvious and the obscure, the fleeting and the eternal, as elements beyond all reckoning of wealth and worth. Sometimes we can still see what is plain to see.

102 Briefly Mentioned, Mostly Living Things

Weddell seal Guinea baboon Waving glass frog Gulf corvina Suraka silk moth Kuhl's pipistrelle Minke whale Humpback whale Giraffe Kate Winslet beetle Bono's Joshua Tree trapdoor spider Humboldt penguin Hog-nosed skunk Greater kudu Lesser kudu Lesser frigatebird Least weasel Least tern Least bittern Serama bantam Jersey Giant ~~Cretan dwarf mammoth~~ ~~Channel Island mammoth~~ Least shrew Lesser earless lizard Lesser sooty owl Lesser mouse-deer ~~Lesser mascarene flying fox~~ ~~Lesser Antillean rice rat Lesser bilby~~ ~~*Giraffatitan brancai Hagryphus giganteus Ugrunaaluk kuukpikensis*~~ Bristlecone pine Peregrine Bhutan glory Diane's bare-hearted glass frog Icelandic cyprine ~~K2~~ ~~*Saurosuchus Dromicosuchus*~~ Wapiti Northern white rhinoceros Eastern brown snake Inland taipan Trinidad Moruga scorpion pepper Komodo dragon pepper Sperm whale Southern elephant seal Cuvier's beaked whale Large-eared pika Yellow-rumped leaf-eared mouse Common swift Brazilian free-tailed bat Cheetah Giant panda Koala Monarch butterfly Raccoon Coyote Peppered moth Sendai crow White clover Madagascar tomato frog Springbok Humpback whale barnacle Crucian carp Naked mole rat Anna's hummingbird Dung beetle Blind cave tetra Hagfish Cuttlefish California two-spot octopus Planarian *Polyommatus* blue butterfly ~~Vladimir Nabokov~~ Pumpkin toadlet Dyeing dart frog Eyelash mite Yellow dent corn *Malus domestica Malus sieversii* Indian giant squirrel Borneo tufted ground

squirrel Clouded leopard Muntjac deer Eastern gray squirrel
Wild mustard Red jungle fowl Cape buffalo Moose Zebra Hip-
popotamus Sumatran rhinoceros Okapi *Takhi Havtagai* Indian
elephant ~~Cave lion Short-faced bear Irish elk~~

The Perfect Party Guest

When deciding on whom to invite to your next gathering, be sure to extend considerations to the sloth. Either the two-toed or three-toed variety will do, as each of these distant relations has unique insights to share concerning their suspensorial lifestyles, which is just a tongue-pleasing way to say upside-down tree living. These days, you needn't even worry about tailoring the invitation like you would eleven thousand years ago, when sloths of the giant and grounded varieties might suddenly show up at your door, not being able to fit through, and wouldn't that be embarrassing, having to turn away guests because the fire code for your condo common room doesn't allow for twelve-foot-tall, elephant-sized vegetarians, and even if it did, you may never live down the fact that your party might be the only in history to run out of salad.

*

Surely, you might protest, there must be others capable of bringing merriment without tracking corn-straw hair and symbiotic algae all over your Berber carpets. Maybe the albatross or the axolotl, as you proceed down your invite list in alphabetical order, or the black marsh turtle, also known as the smiling terrapin, all of whom sound like ideal guests for your shindig. They even sport permanent cheery smiles on their faces, like the sloth. Then you might think—pursuing this glee-based train of thought—that the profile of a bottlenose dolphin may set the perfect tone for a future aquatic-themed celebration, even as you harbor designs for decorating the downstairs pool. You may even be inclined to start working on RSVPs to members of the skate family after hearing about their flap-happy demeanor from the friendly neighborhood ichthyologist, who mentioned one Saturday night that a throng of these round, triangular fish is called a fever, and surely one in the know would base this moniker on late seventies disco vibes.

But just because one is smiling on the outside doesn't mean one weathers untroubled within. Does the psyche of a quokka, dubbed "happiest animal on earth," match the jolly outward expression that made it an Instagram sensation? What storms were brewing inside when it posed so sweetly before biting down on the hand holding a peanut-buttered Wheat Thin? (It is crucial that nobody comes to associate your soirees, which may feature potential finger foods, with the prospect of potential finger loss.) Perhaps the diminutive wallaby was simply overjoyed at the prospect of company, any company, being the lone land mammal on Rottnest Island from whence it came, and overcompensated by coming on a tad strong. I do not know. It is difficult enough to gauge another's mood through the regular assortment of facades; it is even harder when basic anatomy gets in the way. Take the aforementioned skates, with most mistaking their underset nostrils, called nares, for eyes, thus regarding them silly and affable even when they may in reality be sulky and irascible, especially after being made to take time out of their schedule to attend a function unrelated to their dual passions of shell cracking and crab crushing. In this sense, skates might make for better conference delegates than house party invites, as at least on the trade show floor they get to flap their mouths and work the circuit grind without much thought, mirroring what they do in their native benthic habitats anyway.

*

Along a similar vein, don't hold out too much hope for that Antipodean albatross you thought would regale guests with worldly tales of travel. Just because one racks up the air miles doesn't mean they aren't merely going through the motions, like when George Clooney played jet-setting George Clooney in that one movie critics liked but nobody watched. (I feel like there are a lot of these.) Besides being awkward at most land-based affairs, albatrosses are never ones to stick around, always being first to claim that they need to get up early the next morning for a flight bound for some forsaken scrap of rock—usually south of Aotearoa. And not to further dampen the prospect pool, but banter with any axolotl, while bubbly in tone, will always be juvenile in content, for in their state of arrested development, they may only reminisce on days from years past—who dated whom during senior year, which teachers told the worst jokes, and do you remember how they once scored three touchdowns in that state championship game? It may be a depressing exchange in many ways, the saddest of which might be to see someone unable to realize that their best years have passed them by.

And what of the former star performer at many a dolphinarium? Like many a child actor, the bottlenose has long been suffering under the spotlight in captive silence without us realizing it, or perhaps with us denying it, thinking or wishing their playfulness to be jovial in nature, when in reality it was more desperate in form, warped by unfulfilled yearnings for kinship and by desires they themselves do not recall and we cannot even begin to fathom. You will need a much larger space than the downstairs pool for Flipper and his compatriots to feel at ease, so cross them off the invite list, please, for everyone's sake.

*

Yet rounding out that guest list is not a lost cause. The smiling terrapin remains a solid choice, and should you manage to reserve that two-hour block for the pool and jacuzzi combo, be sure to ring up the capybaras, genuine rodents of unusual size and disposition. Unlike other members of its family, which include squirrelly hoarders and mousy scroungers, homebody gophers and workaholic beavers, this mastiff-sized mammal is easygoing and emotionally keen. They can even slot in for you as host should you find yourself overwhelmed, slipping into the murky waters of social exchange with ease, radiating a mellow energy that is likely the result of navigating life in large extended clans. Inviting a capybara is like inviting the most interesting man in the world from those Dos Equis beer commercials but better, because capybaras never spend time boasting about their own exploits—numerous as these are—but instead direct their charisma toward propping up their flock of friends. From the black vulture to the wattled jacana to many a shiny cowbird, the capybara's entourage will attest to the rodent's sturdy character and unmatched sagacity, which lies at the heart of any sound commensal relationship. A lookout perch; a snack bar sporting the finest flies and ticks; complementary ferry service with an onboard sundeck—the capybara is all this and more for its cast of avian companions, is always there to provide.

*

Whomever and whatever you do decide to invite, keep in mind that a memorable party need not be a high-stress event but merely a venue to bring spirits together for connection and communion. In Greece, a group that meets regularly to share their philosophies, values, and ideas is called a *parea*. In Denmark, *hygge* is the term given to a cozy atmosphere cocreated between caring individuals. The allure of the French *salon* stems from it being a space for life-changing conversations. Sometimes the part of the party that truly matters begins in its decline, when the crowd has dwindled and those who came to mooch on potluck and free booze have meandered off. This is the time when the true and few sink into their niches— enveloped by the beanbag in the corner; fortified with cushions around the loveseat; wrapped in a fleece throw, watching the flicker of the woodstove fire. This will be the phase where your sloth guest will start to shine. (Not that it wouldn't have before, being one of the chillest mammals around, body temperature-wise. You would need to suffer from hypothermia to be as cool as a sloth, so don't even try.) Receiving such a relaxed guest naturally means little upkeep and minimal food costs, as the leaf-litter-eater will be glad to divert leftover greens destined for the compost, even those bruised soggy bits you tried to dress up with homemade raspberry vinaigrette. But beyond the dietary and monetary savings, you may be surprised to learn that, beneath its bedraggled exterior, the sloth is a most attentive conversationalist. For one, it has never been known to excuse itself to use the facilities in the middle of an exchange, for it only needs to do its business once a week and seems at peace with the fact that no amount of powder will ever fix that shiny nose. The sloth also excels at defusing those tense situations that threaten to kill the mood of any party, being apt at shedding hurled insults like raindrops off its hirsute coat. For it has long shrugged its way through indignities coming from the peanut gallery, from the drunk by the stairs nobody remembers inviting to snooty eighteenth-century French naturalists like the monkey-loving Count of Buffon, who once out of nowhere besmirched the sloth's good name by decrying it to be "a bungled conformation, the lowest form of existence, and that one more defect would have made its life impossible" (there is more but I shall not reprint any further slander). Such is the sloth's character that even when confronted with such uncouth vitriol, it bore no ill will and would indeed be happy to pick the count's slightly larger than normal-sized brain, now preserved in a crystal urn and installed under his statue at the *Muséum national d'Histoire naturelle*, but only if the chance for a free sightseeing trip to Paris should arise, and only if there is a suitable tree to hang upside down in nearby.

Maybe it is also this tree living that makes the sloth a preferred party guest, for some of the most compelling souls you will ever meet are those who have learned to live arboreally. No, I'm not talking about YouTube survivalists scrounging tubers for the end times, or flannel-wearers building cabins on their parents' vacation properties, but those who have absorbed the art of patience from their tranquil teachers, becoming adept at seeing moments from beginning to end. How a spider weaves its web strand by strand. How the moss around a trunk of a tree swells from dew. What sound is made when a fruiting mushroom breaks the soil surface. The sloth may speak to these and other phenomena throughout the night, should you be inclined to listen. If you are very lucky, it may even speak to trees of the family variety, namely its own, in the stylings of a deep-time saga, full of ancient locutions passed down from sloth to sloth; like the time eight million years ago when its cousins from the genus *Thalassocnus* crossed the Peruvian desert to eke out a sea-grass living, braving waves that threatened to break their bones, and killer whales that threatened to rend their flesh; or when ol' Uncle *Lestodon* from Argentina, a hulking brick of a brute, devoted his life toward spreading avocado trees like a prehistoric Johnny Appleseed while working as a prospector, splitting rocks with nothing but his bare-knuckled claws while digging some of the largest creature-made caves one can find to this day. Your sloth storyteller may decide to insert certain comic interludes— like when its Great-Aunt *Diabolotherium*, whom the locals dubbed "the Devil Beast," got bored of climbing trees and decided one day to scale the Andes instead (whether that was for the view or the thrill, no one knows)—before speaking more solemnly about its house's fall from grace, noting the time of the grinding ice that doomed so many explorers on their North American sojourns. It may describe how some sloths grew in fur and girth to guard against the gnawing frost and saber-toothed cats but found that they could not cope once the climate thawed and warmed once more, even while, as this new world arose, a new threat emerged alongside it, a breed of two-legged hunters against which size and claws proved to be no defense.

*

It is customary for a sloth to buffer its actions with ample bouts of silence, but you may sense this even more so at the end of such an intimate sharing, steeped in an acceptance that its family's gallivanting days are past. The sloth before you, sunken into the floral-patterned velour couch, with one claw hooked around the pisco sour named for the formation where its Peruvian brethren now lie, is one who appears to be done with doing, is at ease with a quieter role on this earth. Perhaps in this case, both the smile it sports and the story it spins are truly as they seem. In the days to follow, you may feel the urge to spend some one-on-one time with the sloth. Do so. For being in the presence of such a soul might help one pick up some much-needed tricks of the heart—namely, how to quiet it down and hold space for the present, and the importance of flipping one's perspective upside down once in a while, so as to gaze out at the world with eyes old yet undiminished.

3. Contact

The fins round goby fish use for perching on rocks are as sensitive as monkey fingertips. Koala fingerprint whorls are so similar to ours that they have the potential to contaminate crime scenes. Koalas, manatees, and European hedgehogs have smooth lissencephalic brains; wombats, camels, and collared peccaries have folded gyrencephalic brains. An elephant's cerebral cortex is twice as heavy as a human's but contains one-third the neurons. The Peters's elephantnose fish has no cortex at all but is able to switch between sensing and seeing processes, like mammals. The remora adheres to its host using a modified head fin made of soft, overlapping ridges called lamellae. The optimal spot for hitchhiking on a cruising whale is either by the blowhole or the dorsal fin, where there is shelter. Flensing is the act of stripping a marine mammal's outer blubber integument from its flesh. No less than 42,698 blue whales were processed on the island of South Georgia between 1904 and 1971. A single new whale sighting was recorded off the island between 1998 and 2018. Fifty-eight were sighted from one survey in 2020. Migration is a form of culture passed down through generations in both bighorn sheep and moose.

A School Is a Type
of Shoal

The very model of a modern sergeant major damselfish is one that sports five stripes narrowing toward the belly and can fall into perfect formation. To shoal together is to sense together, thus making matters animal, vegetal, and mineral simpler to assess. This is useful when navigating craggy reefs filled with crabby denizens, many of whom are keen to nibble on anything animalculous while avoiding being nibbled on in return. Sergeant majors proficient at this synchronized swimming can potentially graduate to schooling, technically a more technical form of shoaling. But while *to shoal* is to be social, which permits some degree of ragtag in makeup and disposition, *to school* together is to sweep in unison together, to glint in the faces of would-be foes together, dazzling them with coherence. This level of coordination demands vigilance—should a silver sprat take its eyes off its closest compatriot, it may find itself suddenly not schooling at all but struck against kin and stricken from the collective, beyond which sailfish, patrolling for truants, may herd it off with sail and speed and stealthiness. If enough eyes are corralled away, the whole school can lose its accreditation, ceasing to possess those emergent benefits afforded from being legion, such as being nigh impossible to capture or comprehend. Even the mightiest major general, flush with brass pips and jangling medals, would flounder against a prowling swordfish if unschooled, for the latter is quick to the draw in the drink, brandishing its bill to disarm even the most accomplished duelist, especially one trying to fight underwater with a wool coat and ceremonial saber.

*

Some in life choose to shoal while some simply never learned not to school. Atlantic cod and Atlantic salmon congregate mostly for spawning reasons, while Pacific herring and Pacific anchovies ball together and forever, partly perhaps because they fear being lonely, partly perhaps because they desire safety. The Krøyer's deep-sea anglerfish neither shoals nor schools, being at home in the abyss, having found a surefire cure for forlorn-ness. When a male anglerfish chances upon a female, he will latch onto her belly with his teeth and dissolve into her being, forfeiting his form and circulatory freedom to become part of her. He trusts that such a union will work out in the end, for it is very difficult for anglerfish to find one another, even with the female sporting a bioluminescent lure. Males are even more minute when counted against the vast schemes of the sea, so seizing upon the first hope to glimmer out of the dark, however faint, is one way to ensure that he will never again be alone, even at the cost of never again being apart.

*

Thus sometimes it avails to be bold, to chance that first step into the unknown and discover something novel, like setting foot on Newfoundland for the first time. Shoring is altogether dif-ferent from shoaling or schooling—so must have sensed *Tik-taalik*, an enterprising fishapod who also set its digits upon the coast of northeast Canada, hoisting itself out of the murk and across mud flats 375 million years ago. While there were others early in the Devonian that could haul themselves ashore with improvised fins, their attempts were tentative, not weight-bearing and hip-driven like *Tiktaalik*'s. To shore surely is to breach the border between worlds, and pressing aground and finding support became central to *Tiktaalik* and all the legged creatures that came subsequently after, whether they chose to amble or gallop or bunny-hop ever forward. Walking under one's own power is an exercise of trust, founded upon a promise made with each raised paw or claw, each lifted hoof or sole, returning always to greet the reliable earth.

*

Of course, there are souls not content to halt their voyage at the one from sea to land, eager to springboard ahead from the ground into the sky. Most still tether themselves to concepts, like familial bonds, or to qualities, like being gregarious, even as they fly farly, forming flocks. Bramblings, also known as mountain finches, gather in the millions to winter on masting Slovenian beeches, taking a page out of their host trees' over-production of nuts to overwhelm would-be snackers through sheer volume. Sparrowhawk locals can only eat so many bramblings—brambling for breakfast, brambling for lunch, brambling all day every day, and still black heads and white rumps and puffed orange chests as far as their keen eyes can see! In this way satiation is a double-edged sword—feeling full can help pace you through lean times, but it can also prevent you from taking full advantage, even when a sudden smorgas-bord descends upon you one day, chirping and a-calling.

Red-billed queleas, on the other hand, are buffet veterans as they migrate across sub-Saharan Africa. Once birds in the back strip bare a section of wild grass or cereal crop, they hopscotch forward to create a new feeding front, forming a conveyer belt that some say resembles a rolling cloud. This would not sound so ominous if queleas were only numerous or only ravenous, but alas they are usually both, with each member of the million-strong swarms able to pack away half its body weight in grain every day. One morning a farmer owns a ripening field of tef or sorghum; the next they own an efficiently sorted one, stowed aboard little bird bellies. What a rain cloud giveth a quelea cloud can taketh away, and neither rage nor flamethrowers nor organothiophosphate poisons seem to make much of a dent in their numbers.

The European starling possesses the ability not only to form clouds of the pesky variety but also poetic ones, which some dub as murmurations. Sometimes starlings are desired for waxing to and upon. Mozart taught the opening melody of the third movement to *Piano Concerto no. 17 in G major* to his pet starling Vogelstar. Samuel Coleridge could not help but describe the morphing shape of a flock flying at dawn over wintry fields as it thickened, deepened, blackened. With such numbers flying in flux over countrysides and city skies, one would think that bird-on-bird collisions would be all-too-common tragedies. But it turns out that each starling's brain only needs to heed three basic rules to keep safe while creating one of nature's most transcendent displays:

- Keep up with its seven closest cousins.
- Give each other a body length or so of space.
- Always veer right if another approaches head-on.

Knowing these tips, you too can enact mass synergies more seamlessly, like if one day you should find yourself in the midst of a marching band or stadium wave, or be tasked with improving anticrash systems for drones whirling about a busying sky. Unfortunately, starlings, clever and myriad as they are, have not yet learned how to murmurate with aircraft, which have proved belligerent to basic avian guidelines. Sixty-two people died in the crash of a Boston Electra in 1960 when the airliner flew into a starling cloud before rolling left (not right) and nose-diving into Winthrop Harbor. A second earlier. A meter more. It is sobering to realize in our daily doings how narrow a margin exists between continuation and calamity. Alas, life, unlike southern flannel moths, does not usually make plain which encounters will leave you pleasantly tickled (the moth form) and which will leave you wracked with pain and ruination (the caterpillar form).

Faced with such uncertainty, the safest course of action may be to eschew contact of any kind—not with outsiders, not with potential venomous larvae, not with any part of the world. Alpine swifts, which resemble kites that have escaped their strings and spindle-holders, can soar alone and aloft for up to seven months at a time on round trips from Switzerland to Mali. If you can dine on the wing and nap on the wing, why risk anything that can perturb your superbly streamlined life? Descent, after all, can only saddle one with complications, like hatchlings that need to be fed seven times a day, or parasitic louse flies that drain your blood and resolve. But perhaps the impulse to ascend forever runs deeper in a creature that converses longer and closer with the heavens than any other. Maybe as a master practitioner of aerodynamics, the swift is also a student of quantum mechanics, recognizing that physical contact is in reality an illusion, cultivated by our senses to register the repulsive forces between our electron configurations and another's. Perhaps the swift has come to terms with the fact that what we tangibly touch is never truly another, but rather the resistance against being occupied, made from shells around shells guarding our innermost cores.

*

This is a tough thought to acknowledge, especially for those accustomed to marching and schooling and flocking in solidarity. But while it might be true that we resemble the shy crowns of Borneo camphor trees more than we care to admit, ever branching toward each other but never touching in canopy, other agents may yet sway us. For the ties that bind need not be material. In a universe with so much gap and so much void, there exists a phenomenon that draws together everything from everywhere. Some call this gravity. Others call it love. To love is to beckon in spirit. To love is to come together. Gravity may prove to be the most patient form of love, outlasting the stars and their fires, outlasting light and its fleetingness. The only thing it cannot fully capture might be time, although it tries its best to slow it down, which is sometimes what it feels like to be in love.

Gravity is very potent within the embrace of a neutron star, where atoms are compacted down to be as close as anything can get without risking collapse. Under such pressures we may wish for the opposite of what we formerly desired, aching to fling ourselves far and free like fleeing radio waves, to beam our relief outward at having escaped such intense adoration, such fathomless faithfulness. Such is the tragedy of being beings that are whole and complex and contradictory. We lament about not being able to connect, yet cannot bear the thought of being subsumed. Perhaps what we truly crave lies in the act of encircling, to orbit one another around an unspoken center, apart but never parting, never fully merging so we can be constant in our yearning, to touch, to commune, as points of a constellation-in-making.

A Hearth Is a Kind of Home

The King may sway and sing of home being where the heart is, but for some it's the reverse that holds the appeal. To ensconce one's being and belongings inside a portable palace is the dream of any aspiring RV owner or singing scallop. Oh, to visit odd-poriums in Delaware one afternoon and then New Jersey road-side elephants the next! To hinge-hinge-jet away at three in the morning when unscrupulous sea stars come a-prying! There may be no freer living than roaming the open road or sea, heeding only the words of wind or wave that the world can indeed be your oyster, as long as you never settle down like one.

*

Should you fare more oyster than scallop, are more salaried and sedentary, take comfort in the fact that there exist home-bodies even less uprootable than you. Some have never left their abode, not even if they lived to the ripe age of 168, like one Pacific geoduck did before being dug up unceremoniously. Entrenched beneath silt and sea, this giant clam most likely never gave a second thought (or a first) toward moving out of its drab shell, even though its three-foot elephantine siphon outgrew its eight-inch home decades back. Then there is the giant Aldabra tortoise, who spends its triple-digit lifespan in the same shell patrolling the same atoll, tending to its turf blend of twenty herbs and grasses, gazing out at the Indian Ocean. There is attachment to one's childhood home, and then there is having it directly fused to your spine and ribs. While this may mean that a tortoise need never worry about being eaten out of carapace and plastron, it also means that most travel accidents it suffers will double as at-home mishaps (tortoise insurance claims must be simpler to process and then deny). Baked alive by the equatorial sun if it cannot lug itself into shade or cave; flipped over by seventeenth-century sailors seeking respite from bad beef and hardtack—woe to be the architect of one's own nonventilatable and easily tippable doom! Worse might be to trundle on through the years with no hope of a refresh in decor. There are timeless styles and then there is tortoise scute mosaic. Luckily, fashion trends are fickle, and nostalgia for upper-class, Roman-inspired stylings may circle back around one day and make tortoiseshell happen again.

*

For those unmoved by the sweet succor of childhood spaces and bygone times, the challenges and stresses of finding a new home may weigh heavier in mind. In an ideal world, landlords would let you try a suite on for size, to see if the kitchen color scheme works in the afternoon light, or whether the den has enough space for both you and your untoted possessions. Purple pincher hermit crabs sometimes test-drive homes at impromptu swap meets, with up to twenty individuals showing up to form a conga line of descending size around one prospective shell. Once the Goldilocks crab claims its new Goldilocks home, the rest of the house-swapping frenzy can commence and conclude in seconds. In an ideal world, this social arrangement known as a vacancy chain would have everyone coming away with extra square inch-age, but often the shell game lives up to its name, with unlucky hermit crabs clamped out of their homes and left even more bereft than their human mountain counterparts. There may be as many regretful shell swappers as there are remorseful home buyers in this world; instead of griping about losing out on that dream duplex with the deluxe carport, the crustacean might rue the day it gave up its chestnut turban haunts in favor of the hot-pink murex affair, which seemed to have everything going for it, except for coziness. Luckily, hermit crabs harbor no notions of shame or economic theory, having been known to scoot back and forth between multiple dwellings, unlike those of us locked into what in Law French means a "death pledge," so long as the coast is clear and the former residence remains decapod-free.

*

Those house-savvy and home-handy enough to scoop up fixer-uppers should look once more to the crustacean world for tips on refurbishment. Graceful decorator crabs attach to their shells strawberry anemones (which are not really strawberries and not really anemones—such is the depth of their subterfuge), while furred sponge crabs cover their backs with snipped bits of living sponges. The latter's action is similar to installing a regular roof, except a sponge roof shields instead of attracts curious eyes while offering the same noxious surprise for curious mouths, as anyone who has ever munched on a spiculated sponge or duroid shingle can attest. The downside to going down this rabbit hole of self-renovation is that it might pave the way to self-crankification. Even old friends inclined to stop by for a visit will find you difficult to locate or to stomach, what with your dwelling so

thoroughly disguised and distasteful that they may leave you to
your own devices for good.

                                    *

Those lacking in motivation or coordination may wish to sub-
scribe to the quarterly magazine of the French Conchologist As-
sociation. Within each issue you can admire home after home,
all crafted sans hands or digits of any kind. While thus being
comforted you can also become inspired by the genus group of
carrier snails responsible for the publication's title, *Xenophora*.
Carrier snails have one core philosophy when it comes to home-
building: Why spend energy crafting when there are free ma-
terials for the taking? Why drive down to the hardware store
and pay for lumber when you can attach the neighbor's shed to
your burgeoning bungalow? Carrier snails cement anything
and everything to their shell whorls as they grow. No need to
decide between a new solarium or kitchen island or backyard
jungle gym—you can have it all, one next to the other! Whether
nearby clams and pebbles mind being fused together is of little
concern to a xenophorid conglomerate, and while such a haphazard approach to construction might not hold up to building
codes and accessibility guidelines, if the fire risks are limited
where you live (like underwater) and your neighbors are gos-
sipy gulps keen to gobble up any news or parts of you, radiating
rocks and shards and pleated bottle caps may work better than
any "Beware of Dog" sign ever could (especially underwater).

Of course, kleptomania can be anathema not only to the
aggrieved. Those determined to build their home on the up-
and-up may wish to consult with their local white-nest swiftlet
design firm. Each bonded pair pours more than sweat and tears

into their artisanal homes, weaving nests out of 100 percent self-sourced saliva, which spools from their mouths into sticky noodle fibers before air-drying on walls. But it might be best to only chat and not commission a project; swiftlet designer homes are in high demand, with wealthy clients even building buildings to house more birds so the birds can build more nests. This naturally means that the going rates are exorbitant, to the point that their nests are no longer worth the asking price, being bland in taste and overly cramped for living. If you must splurge on a luxury home made of luxury spit, consider a manuka honey hive, a far more nutritious and rewarding bargain by comparison.

*

Should one day your wildest fortunes come to fruition, and budget poses no barrier to your grandest ambitions, some lavishness and extravagance may be merited or even expected of your primary residence. From English estates of yore to modern-day McMansions, there are no shortages of palatial templates to emulate. But exercise caution, especially if you sport the obsessive personality of mollusks and are predisposed to chase spiral visions of Fibonacci perfection. Avoid making the mistakes the House of Ammonite did. Once builders of the most avant-garde, multichambered shells, ammonites created ram spirals and coiled snakes before there were rams or snakes, crafted shapes of shoehorns and paper clips before they became common household objects. But designing a fancy buoyant home can be the key to your success and the key to your doom. You can feast on the top richest layers of the sea to your blue-blooded hearts' content, growing as fat as monster truck tires. Yet the security the shell offers can also prevent you from evolving new ways to be, such as learning to live more deeply, which might have helped the ammonites when the asteroid that wiped out the dinosaurs struck; or learning to live more thriftily, which would have helped the ammonites wean off their mineral inheritance during times of carbonate recession, when even the very seas began to sour. It may be in poor taste and judgment to fault ammonites for their extravagance—our own species will most likely not live through one mass extinction, let alone three. But there is something tragic about seeing a layer of ammonites swimming in a cliff face instead of out at sea, knowing that their legacy is now forever locked in the stony past, with no present-day relations willing to take up the old mantle. Modern cephalopods desire no baggage, preferring the mobility to move up and down ocean stratums without succumbing to pressures either ancestral or aquatic. Whatever vestiges remain most now house in secret: the pharaoh cuttlefish keeps its cuttlebone deep within and out of sight; the neon flying squid sheaths its bequeathed gladius under its hood; the seven-armed octopus seems keen to pawn away even its last remnant pair of shell stylets in favor of flexibility in all forms (even in truth, for it actually sports eight arms). Only the chambered nautilus still wears its shell banner. But it is only a cousin's cousin to the original ammonite lineage, and should the ancient mariner ever attempt to restore the house's grandeur, it would likely be seen as an anachronism more than it already is, a fossil out of time and place, a pauper's claimant to a throne best left forgotten.

*

While there are those who still wish to seize the chance to rule, most of us, if bestowed such a reign, would feel like Napoleon Bonaparte inside Longwood House, small and proud but antsy, rocking on the porch chair, scanning ships that pass by the isle of St. Helena, cutting holes in the window shutters to spy on unfair overseers, reliving past victories in the anteroom and the theatre of the mind. Shelter can shield deposed emperors partially against damp chills and plateau winds but not at all against boredom, against loneliness. Perhaps this is why sociable weaver birds of the southern Kalahari, non-exiled and anti-autocratic, band together in numbers and across generations. Their haystack-style compound nests on telephone poles and acacia trees may contain up to a hundred chambers, assembled like a sort of honeycombed B&B. (Daily breakfast consists of juicy harvester termites with a side of termite juice.) A sociable weaver nest can last ten times longer than a sociable weaver bird, which means that running the family enterprise is a full-time venture: no summer vacations, no mass migrations. Outside of this shortcoming, it might seem that this exercise in communal living, unique among birds, is idyllic in all the ways that matter. Consider a perched location with prime views; private rooms that stay cool during the afternoon boil and cozy through the night chill; siblings and offsprings constantly available for egg-sitting or cleanup duties; fulfilling chats (the conversations) with familiar chats (the birds), sprinkled with doses of gossip with visiting rosy-faced lovebirds. What more could one ask for in a life and a home? But like any cooperative, this living arrangement can be rife with internal drama, and if one could decipher weaver chatter, a large part of it would likely come across as grievances. How birdbrain there forgot to install straw spikes at the entrance and let the cape cobra in. How the tree skinks have been eavesdropping and decoding the secret alarm system. Too many impalas napping under the tree. Too many cheetahs lounging on the roof. OH GOD HONEY BADGER HONEY BADGER HONEY BADGER. Then there is the whole live-in situation with the pygmy falcon. A raptor a day might keep the boomslangs away, but when times and lizards are lean, the sentry guard with a family to feed can turn birdnapper, snatching up weaver chicks and even an adult or two. Yet for all their incessant nattering, the weaver community is generous to a fault, being loath to evict their obligate dependents. "To turn them out? In this economy?" So they chirp and debate and usually relent. Perhaps these sparrow-sized homemakers realize how much easier it is to tear down a community than to build one up, and to defy the multitude of forces that gnaw at the fabric of society takes not only communication and vigilance but also, on occasion, a quality of mercy.

*

In the end, a home is forged through inhabitation. Gravitas, Apollo & Associates may have accreted stardust into rocky planets, but tenant quality is a big reason why Earth remains lively while Mars has gone to rust. Diligent renters like asparagus ferns and phytoplankton can infuse a space with literal feng shui regardless of placement, while members of the mycelial network are the most cleanliness-obsessed caretakers you shall ever find, being matter-breaker-downers by trade. To be sure, there are loud and noisy denizens like howler monkeys and greengrocer cicadas, but no one minds overmuch, really, especially when they tend to throw the best block parties (the latter's coming-out celebration is always worth the seven years' wait). Besides, who can fault puna flamingos and boreal chorus frogs and screaming hairy armadillos for being a bit raucous after securing leases on a planet so lush, so oxygenated, so amenable to rewroughting?

Yet there are those that do not recognize their privilege, like helium, who has never shown interest in any posted planetary processes or neighborhood functions, sans the occasional children's birthday party. Helium released from balloons and voice boxes eventually finds itself in space, always friendless, always adrift. It seems that only the sun can offer helium a home; only the sun is sufficient enough to give it purpose. But helium's epiphany will take so long to occur that when it happens, the sun will stop looking like the sun and horses will stop looking like horses (though tuataras may still look like tuataras). As the sun exhausts its hydrogen stores, it will task helium to take over the entire solar operation. At such pressure, helium will finally relent, shouldering the shine while fusing into carbon, that prized ingredient that will one day comprise the hearts of new inhabitants on new worlds. But this noble turnabout will come too late to mean anything to its former neighbors on its former world, having all moved on and forgotten helium's name, or names in general.

*

Back in the present, there will be always a few trouble tenants that slip through, like trapdoor spiders and human beings, walling up inside their rooms and becoming too engrossed in their machinations to notice much else. Of course, most arachnid schemes do not compare to our current efforts to turn the earth into a Venus Mark II (Two Venuses? In the same solar system?), which is bad news for those who dislike having their carbon dioxide concentrations increased a hundredfold or their rains to be sulfuric or their winters to reach oven-broil temperatures. The shame is that most of us besides leadsmiths would also prefer a cooler, greener, nonrunaway Earth, would love to share this space more amicably with Australian tree ferns and leafy seadragons and pleasing fungus beetles. We truly do. But to that end, we may need to expand our consideration as we have already expanded our consumption: circularly, outward to encompass the welfare of all dwelling on this Gaia block. For living well with others means being a good neighbor, and if we can learn to get along with the star-nosed mole under the radish patch and the pumpkinseed fish in the lily pond and the Rasberry crazy ants inside the electrical box, we might be able to steer away from a regret-filled helium-esque future and toward one where home and heart can come together to form a hearth, a space where all can thrive, with room to romp, with room for splendor.

4. Exchange

Florida carpenter ants use the formic acid they produce for defense to disinfect their insides. The process by which turkey vultures excrete on their feet to clean and cool them down is called urohidrosis. Human stomach pH values are closer to those of carrion feeders than to carnivores or omnivores. Chimps parasitized with toxoplasmosis are drawn to the scent of the urine of leopards, their chief predator. Researchers have formally described the all-purpose cloacal vent of a one-hundred-million-year-old *Psittacosaurus*: the area around the dinosaur's backside, highly pigmented with melanin, was likely used for display and signaling, like the rump of a male baboon. Melanin on the bodies of sixteen species of deep-sea fishes provides "ultra-black" camouflage that absorbs more than 99.5 percent of incoming light. *Fritillaria delavayi*, a bright green flower used in traditional Chinese medicine, evolved brown and gray foliage to make it less visible on mountains with human harvesting pressures. The African puff adder employs chemical crypsis to avoid being sniffed out by dogs and meerkats. Lions can spot zebra outlines as well as they can topis, waterbucks, and wildebeests, but horseflies struggle with landing on striped bodies compared to unstriped ones. Bumblebees can sense, discern, and alter the electric fields of flowers they visit. A quarter of wild bee species have gone missing from public records since the 1990s.

A Breath in Four Parts

1. Inhale

An African elephant's trunk can create suction exceeding the speed of the Shinkansen. Reindeer noses can raise the temperature of incoming air by eighty degrees in less than a second. The convoluted sinuses of rhino-sized ankylosaurs may have served as air conditioners for cooling their walnut-sized brains. The inflatable nostrils of saiga antelopes may have evolved to filter dust clouds generated during their mass migrations. Two-thirds of the global saiga population died in 2015 due to bacterial nasal infections. Myanmar snub-nosed monkeys sit with their heads between their knees when it rains to avoid getting water in their nostrils and sneezing. Sternutation is a biological response to reboot the nasal chamber after being overwhelmed with stimuli. *The American Journal of Rhinology and Allergy* cataloged fifty-two unique cases of sneezing-related injuries between 1948 to 2018. "Holding it in" can increase pressure on internal airways by over 2,000 percent. Biologists injected drugs to trigger sneezes in freshwater sponges to understand how creatures without nervous systems respond to their environment. Researchers have recently described fossilized pollen in explosive mid-discharge from its flower.

2. Respire

A cheetah can take 150 breaths per minute while in full sprint. One distinguishing feature of mammals is the presence of a flexible diaphragm muscle. Approximately four thousand people in the United States are hospitalized for hiccups each year. Intractable hiccups are defined as cases lasting more than a month. In clinical studies, pigs and mice have shown the ability to breathe through their intestines. Dojo loaches and peppered catfish can absorb oxygen through their hindguts while in anoxic environments. The Mary River turtle, also known as the green-hair turtle, also known as the bum-breathing turtle, possesses gill-like structures near its cloaca that allow it to lie submerged for days. Trilobite fossils preserved in fool's gold reveal well-developed gills on their upper leg branches. The Borneo flat-headed frog is the first recorded frog to have no lungs, breathing exclusively through its skin. A ten-celled parasitic relative of jellyfish living in salmon muscle is the first documented animal to have no need to breathe at all.

3. Suspend

Apnea can be defined as the temporary hiatus of breathing. Gray seal pups that are more keen to play in pools of water become better at holding their breath as adults. Some marine mammals can "download" oxygen directly into their skeletal muscles to stay active longer underwater. The Bajau people of Southeast Asia, or the sea nomads, possess enlarged spleens as an adaptation to their free-diving lifestyles. The water anole of Costa Rica can attach a bubble to the top of its head as a makeshift scuba tank. American alligators can shift the internal positions of their lungs to perform silent underwater maneuvers: backward to dive, forward to surface, and sideways to roll. The deep-sea coffinfish is the first documented fish to hold its breath in water for up to four minutes. Grasshoppers routinely stop breathing through their spiracles to reduce oxidative damage to their tissues. Researchers use obese Yucatan miniature pigs to study obstructive sleep apnea. Vibrations generated by heavy snoring can damage the upper respiratory airways and inhibit healing processes. Training breast cancer patients to perform five-minute breath holds can increase the precision of radiation therapy. Weddell seal pups need to breathe every six minutes when first learning to navigate under Antarctic ice sheets. A common cause of death among young seals is drowning from being unable to reach a breathing hole in time.

4. Exhale

Ancient volcanic eruptions may have fertilized coastal areas and allowed the first oxygen-producing lifeforms to flourish. Life may have metabolized nitrous oxide, or laughing gas, during the period in Earth's history known as "the Boring Billion." The time of the Permian mass extinction may have also been the smelliest, as microbes expelled hydrogen sulfide into the atmosphere. Physicists have been able to recreate laboratory versions of solar winds along with the plasma "burps" that fuel them. Evidence points to traces of a massive carbon dioxide release deep within the Southern Ocean at the end of the last Ice Age. King penguin colonies release prodigious amounts of nitrous oxide, or laughing gas, in their droppings. Feeding cattle seaweed supplements can significantly reduce the methane they generate from belching and flatulence. Unlike human adults, human babies laugh both as they inhale and exhale, similar to chimpanzees. Belugas have been observed to blow four types of bubbles through their mouths and blowholes, mostly for fun.

How to Make Friends
and Keep Them Lifelong

Perhaps while penning *How to Win Friends and Influence People*, motivational speaker Dale Carnegie was working out his own difficulties in forging new connections. Maybe what came so easily to him through child's play and college days seemed to entail extra effort as an adult. Should you too find yourself mired in the doldrums of home and work life, craving new friendships but unsure where to begin, take heart in the first quote of the first chapter of Carnegie's perennial bestseller and start gathering honey by visiting (and not kicking over) your local beehive. This is because apiaries are bustling hubs teeming with souls so convivial that Dr. Suzanne Batra had to coin the term *eusocial* in 1966 to capture such advanced levels of chumminess. Who you wish to eusocialize with is of course your business, but befriending a honeybee can bestow benefits beyond the direct sweet reward. Taking jaunts together you may learn to see old neighborhoods in a new light, moving not rectilinearly along gridded streets and sequential shopfronts but spottily, selectively, following diaphanous trails of seasonal blooms. Here an early snowdrop, there a delectable dandelion! Here heady lilacs and summer lavender, there nodding onions and brilliant bachelor's buttons! And should you ever wish to take up dancing, look no further than your companion to instruct you on that art most sublime. You might be tempted to read up on the stylings of *Tanzsprache* beforehand, that bee language that does double duty as bee communiques, but there is no need. Chances are your dance partner won't be expecting your limited limbs to pick up what Austrian ethologist Ritter von Frisch spent a lifetime attempting to decipher. Simply waggle-whirl in figure eights and have a good time. The summer span of a worker bee lasts a mere six weeks, and surely she would enjoy a spot of reprieve in your brief while together.

*

For longer lasting associations, try reaching out to those who share your interests. These acquaintances need not be question-naired and found compatible on multiple dimensions; they can simply be occasional fellows with which you can do activities together. A common sport can be a solid icebreaker, as doing does more to kindle kinship than idle chitchat. Go bouldering with your neighborhood North American mountain goat. Take up hang-gliding with a local Philippine colugo. Try fly-shooting with the chapter of banded archerfish at your nearby brack-ish lagoon. That said, be mindful of your comfort and commit-ment level before embarking on such excursions, especially with amateur athletes dedicated enough to evolve cloven hooves for climbing or full-body membranes for tree-sailing, or who have devoted their youths to honing trick shots that account for the refractive angle between water and air. Should you be genu-ine in your pursuit of mutual passions, these serious masters can grow into lifelong comrades, teachers, and confidants, all rolled into one. But should you find yourself wavering at such intense demands of body and spirit, remember that there are plenty of fish to shoot the breeze (and not bugs) with. There is no shame in seeking more casual affairs. No one should pretend to be who they aren't for the sake of maintaining a friendship, lest one day you find yourself abandoned on a sixty-degree incline thirteen thousand feet up by whom you thought was your best bud and GOAT companion, lamenting not just joining the local pickleball league—even though that one guy yells after every overhead—realizing in hindsight that it might not have been wise to spend so much time with someone whose hobby was their sole enterprise.

*

Accept fickleness and failure in friendships. Accept that not every connection will work out, that some will sputter out shortly after ignition, while others may sour slowly across the years, and not the tasty kind of souring, like the tender, patient relationship you cultivated with the mother of vinegar fermenting on the kitchen counter, that living acetobacterial conglomerate that offers so much zest and complexity to an otherwise simple sugar life. No, I'm referring to toxic encounters akin to the botulistic sort, where even the most minute exposure can poison your mood and constitution. Severing these paralytic ties may be the best thing you can do for yourself, like how we as a species cut things off with smallpox—good riddance—or more recently with rinderpest, much to the relief of gaurs and warthogs and all our hoofed compatriots out there.

But what if you, YOU, were the offending party? This is a hard thing to bear. Who among us in our youths did not harbor shameful indiscretions, when we so stupidly drove away those decent influences in our lives, failing to see their kindness and wisdom on offer? Take our fraught relations with the American bison. How we took them for granted, believing there to be no limits to their generosity. Year after year, we took and took, as food and shelter, for clothing and cruel sport, until one day, after sixty million souls had dwindled to 541, they had enough and cantered off. It is no wonder that bison remain wary, even as we try to make our meager amends at redress. You cannot blame them. There are some hurts that cannot be mended, like that which we inflicted upon the passenger pigeon, draining a three-billion flock of goodwill down to one lonesome bird named Martha, who then proceeded to ghost us a century ago by dying unforgiving. Confronting our past bad behavior may be painful, but it may also be necessary for forging healthier relationships going forward. We can either learn from our former transgressions or not. We can either strive to be better in the future or not.

*

Perhaps while remembering dead branches that were never to be, you come to ponder the fates of those with whom you were once as thick as thieves, all of whom now range beyond your social spheres, as distant as beaked whales dwelling in the Southern Ocean. How nice it would be to catch up over a few pints and plates of calamari with Arnoux and Andrew, Hector and Sato! But always it seems some circumstance of scheduling stymies you from reforging those bonds, as remote now as beaked whales of the same names dwelling in the Southern Ocean, where the next-closest human dwelling lies not in a cardinal direction but an orbital one, skyward up at the International Space Station.

So instead of traversing far, you may choose to delve back, Facebook-checking those whose paths diverged from yours long ago, when you left home to travel the world and they stayed put to lay down roots. This is similar to what happened with those in the mammalian clade Afrotheria (which translates to "the Wild Beasts of Africa," the name of many a high school hair-metal band). Members include the rock-dwelling hyrax and the grub-munching tenrec, both of whom have never stepped paw beyond their birthplace continent and are now overshadowed by their cosmopolitan brethren, like the dugong and the elephant, with the latter going on to shine so bright that one member, the elephant shrew, was forced to rebrand itself as the sengis, even though, locally, everyone knew it was the first to rock that iconic snout.

Recalling the fate of past friends might dredge up some sadness, some melancholy. But it is not fruitful to dwell on the hows and whys of lives drifting apart. Camaraderie is so often founded on and dissolved by fate, like how perhaps one day you struck a chord with someone at the nearby watering hole, a place you both treasured for its enticing snacks and diverse patrons, but then later discovered you could never connect outside that specific locale, which eventually shuttered due to changes in climate and clientele. This can happen despite genuine efforts to make things work, like you proposing the beach as a new regular hangout spot. For chemistry is a capricious thing, and beaches can be shifty places of divergence, border worlds alive with their own dramas and allures. So the common ancestors to golden moles and manatees might have discovered long ago, with one being drawn to the scent of salt and the curl of waves, while the other worried their toes into toasty grains of sand. This might have been all it took to spell the end of their time together, as one heeded the siren call of seagrass, never to return ashore, while the other burrowed under to forge a life beneath the dunes. Here is not the last time where subtle shifts in preferences drove permanent partings over time, which is technically speciation in a nutshell, that force always lurking at the fringes, threatening to sunder all forms of fellowship.

*

How fragile these links! How tenuous each relation! All the more reason to cherish the connections that do sprout forth, to nurture those leggy saplings into sturdy oaks. But such sowing and tending comes easier for some than others. If you are an extrovert, it might behoove you to reach out to those who tend to direct their energies internally. Certain fine friends can be as shy as silver-backed chevrotains, so averse to interactions that twenty-nine years might pass between sightings, and even then it might only be through the use of camera traps, which comes across a bit stalkerish. Yet without such aggressive solicitations, we would know even less about this lovely creature alongside other cool cats, like those of the African golden variety, which may only show up once after four years of constant party invitations, or those of the Nepalese leopard variety, usually too busy doing some stalking of their own for blue sheep and wild ibex. Even if the entity locally known as the *Heung chituwa* refuses to grace you with its presence, it may still make a strong impression through its absence, as it did on the late writer Peter Matthiessen, who devoted an entire book and pilgrimage toward his nonsighting of the ghostly feline. "Have you seen the snow leopard?" he writes. "No! Isn't that wonderful?"

*

At this reminder of the precarity of encounters, you may harken back to certain rendezvous where it seemed like you were destined to meet and meet intensely, but at the cost of doing so once and once only—think a real-life version of Sophia Coppola's *Lost in Translation*, except with less Bill Murray singing karaoke, less zigzagging through Shibuya Crossing. This proved the case for Captain Guy Chester Shortridge, who spotted the only Visagie's golden mole on record one day at Gouna in South Africa, and for Frederik Hendrik Endert when he came across a lone specimen of the velvet pitcher plant on Mount Kemul in Borneo. And behind every *Osedax mucofloris* success story lies a single improbable union, for no bone-eating snot-flower worm can amount to much without a meeting with a whale carcass on the seafloor. With such a find comes the worm's entire life purpose; through its breakdown of blubber and bone, it graduates into the architect of an oceanic oasis that nourishes riffraff from across the abyssal plains. Such is the power of a single meeting between worm and whalefall, fate-touched, miraculous. If one is indeed the loneliest number, as stated by the main song and theme in P. T. Anderson's *Magnolia*, yet another turn-of-the-century film featuring the intersection of wayward souls, then perhaps every encounter can be seen as a redemption, a staving-off against obscurity and being forgotten, whether it lasts a second or a lifetime. Here, two souls mingle awhile before drifting apart. Changed.

*

Ultimately, it may be this resonance that we crave, us with our collection of cells so permeable to the world, so hungry to find beyond our borders another's hand to pull us across the void. When the little prince accepts the fennec fox's offer to tame each other among the wheat fields in Antoine de Saint-Exupery's most famous fable, the boy becomes more than just a boy, and the fox becomes more than just a fox. And even if this special status does not endure, Saint Ex—as he was known to his friends in real life—waxed about its significance in *Wind, Sand and Stars*, his less known but no less beautiful memoir.

Should you, too, be lucky enough to possess such a friendship, keeping it hale and stout across the decades, you may begin to understand something of what the little prince and the fox felt at their final farewell. How even as their ways part, they can shed tears and smile true, knowing that each has imbued the other with meaning for a spell, knowing how each has tempered the other for their journeys ahead, alone yes but never really, soothed in spirit always by that familiar wind whistling through their shared fields of yesteryear, conjured from memory at need, just so.

Life Lessons from the
Odd and Ancient

If you've been feeling rudderless on the sea of life lately, it might be best to drop anchor and seek guidance from an elder. You may wish to fish one out of the drink, like Captain Hendrik Goosen did one salty morning off the coast of South Africa in 1938, but be sure to verify its credentials, as Marjorie Courtenay-Latimer did after noting the creature's four fleshy fins and puppy-dog tail. Surprised at being consulted after four hundred million years, the coelacanth may be inclined to impart its accrued wisdom onto receptive devotees. It may decide to reveal its technique for weathering the world's turnings even while others succumb to voguish whims, like stretching lobes into hooves and fins into wings, all ventures it surmised, after much fathoming, lead only to speciated partings and premature ruination. The venerable fish may choose to convey this knowledge not so much in words, for its brain is too fat-addled to form them, and its mouth is more for hinging wide than speaking long, but through the shimmers of its chain-mail carriage, adamant against change, against sorrow. Delve deep. Hold fast. Stay true, even when the world has forsaken you.

*

If the coelacanth's teachings seem detached and less than revelatory, you may wish instead to commune with a more accessible and terrestrial spirit. You can often find one standing by nearby sidewalks, contemplating bird songs and diesel fumes, for the ginkgo tree is equally at home in Zen monasteries or downtown urban cores. Learning his life story may leave you awestruck by his steadfastness in nature and purpose, by his gumption to forge his own way a quarter of a billion years ago. "There is nothing new under the sun," swayed Cousin Cycad and distant conifer relations, "green and evergreen is all there is and all there shall ever be!"—to which the teenage Ginkgo, self-assured even back in the Permian, responded by unfurling his maiden mane of luminous gold, astonishing an age still oblivious to sheddable showiness or autumnal melancholy. Nothing since has matched the audacity of that initial feat, not even the subsequent waves of floral trends that have come to drown the earth. The flowering plants dare not try, knowing that their faunal collaborations, while fruit-bearing and crowd-pleasing, pale in intensity against the ginkgo's clarity of vision, distilled in the sculpted lobes of each fan-shaped leaf.

*

By now you may think that to live geologically is to live solitarily, and you might be right, for there are many outlastings during one's long-lasting. To avoid a terminal case of forlornness, some ancients have chosen to radiate freely, like turtles. Turtles, like jazz masters, pride themselves on both their solid fundamentals and their knack for improvisation: a shell standard plus flippers to scull-scull the seas; a shell propped on piano legs to stride highlands and drylands; a shell tipped with siren tongue and beaky maw to lure and snatch passing curios or curious passersby. Yet while the shell may be a turtle essential, it limits not a turtle's potential; from carapaced conformity flows forth surprising creativity, both of which can combine to forge a lasting solidarity, so that in the event a turtle lineage strays off course, onto lonesome islands where sudden goats appear to steal its shrubs, or onto sandy beaches where sudden resorts arise to steal its nights, turtle conventions shall still abound, filled with red-eared slidings and yellow-bellied stackings, rowdy with alligator snappings and leatherback belchings, proudly proclaiming to the world that turtles exist, that they are very old, that they are not alone.

*

Perhaps for you, simply living long and living known is not enough. Perhaps you crave guidance on how to charge ahead with confidence and certainty. For this counsel you may wish to confer with sharks, who learned long ago to streamline their lives and hone their skills to carve out a niche anywhere, from the muddiest bottom to the loftiest apex. Like coelacanths, sharks are laconic, preferring to save their mouths for more gustatory forms of interactions. Yet face-to-face encounters may still prove illuminating, for sharks shed their enamel as they nibble and network, casting teeth about like business cards. Examine one closely and you may glean a pertinent life philosophy. The flattened cusps from a zebra shark may advise that you be persistent in your endeavors, that muscular determination will grind down the barriers between you and your dreams. The needlepoints from a shortfin mako on the other hand, might urge you to pin down prime prospects, silvery and slippery as they are, and never let go. Then there come the jagged triangles from a great white, which may reveal that the key for tackling large life goals is to saw them off into chunks so that each task becomes digestible, even without chewing.

But beware, for not all sharks are success sharks. Some, like the basking variety, possess vestigial teeth that yield vestigial advice—like now is a grand time to get into door-to-door encyclopedia sales—while its laze-about lifestyle can set a poor example for those seeking life guidance, like many a reader of this essay still wondering whether it will lead anywhere. (Be patient, like the part-shark, part-carpet tasselled wobbegong.) Others, like the cookie-cutter shark, may leave you feeling queasy on the inside and perforated on the outside, being known to gouge rounds out of the unsuspecting torsos of bony fish, doughy seals, and rubbery submarines. One should not judge it too harshly. If *you* were birthed into the world as a cigar with a bandsaw in your mouth, you would be wise to make do with your God-given gifts. Besides, infamy may be a desirable trait, and reputation can sometimes last as long as teeth.

*

Still, no matter how notorious you become, one day you too shall be gone, like the ammonites described in a past essay, those marine mollusks who in their shuffling off this mortal coil left behind many exquisite ones. Even the deeds you thought most enduring will come across as fleeting in hindsight, especially when compared to trilobite feats, which were even earlier and grander than ammonite acts, while your contributions will pale when measured against either group, if only for the fact that squishy remains do not preserve as well as spiral shells or chitinous exoskeletons. There is no sense trying to live up to trilobites, by the way; simply accept that they were the first to see everything and the best at spreading everywhere, having evolved complex eyes to find their way from the shallowest shores to the deepest abyss. Those still keen to flee their collective shadow by leaving the seas and climbing skyward should know that it is a futile exercise, as trilobites stamped their mark on Earth's highest peak long ago, back when Oklahoma was near Morocco and both were popular trilobite hangouts, and they managed to do this without the need for crampons or oxygen masks, just by summiting smartly, long before Everest harbored any ambitions of becoming mountain. It is a good thing that trilobites are proactive but not boastful. Otherwise we would hear no end of their past exploits, which would inevitably lead to laments of past regrets, as those trapped in their own calcareous glories may wish to dwell.

*

Realizing that nothing one does will amount to much can prove deflating for those committed to the road of self-betterment. But instead of questing for the future, perhaps this can be a lesson on focusing on the present. For such insights you will need to consult a clown, for unlike sages and visionaries focused on detachment and enlightenment, or peers and professionals obsessed with belonging and success, the fool sees clear into the absurd heart of life. Take the red panda, an old soul stuffed into adorable attire, lonely in lineage but showy for company, a prissy groomer who is always game for tramping and traipsing. All it seems to want in life is some bamboo for munching, a tree for dangle-footed napping, perhaps a pumpkin for pouncing practice. (Save the YouTube video of this for your darkest and most insignificant-feeling day.) Even as it diminishes in the cloud forests of western China and across the Himalayas, balancing above precipices real and existential, its white masked face betrays no signs of worry. Perhaps the red panda does not understand its predicament. Or perhaps it grasps all fates, all fadings, accepting them entire, and so regards each second as an eon, reveling in the honeyed warmth of the morning sun, the bright savor of each spring shoot, the wrapped bliss self-supplied by its ringed and russet tail. If we can heed this guide and embrace our doom as it does by standing tall with arms raised in the most open and heart-melting of poses we shall have secured a very great secret.

5. Duress

Garden-center neonicotinoid pesticides can disrupt the circadian rhythms of insects. White-nose syndrome starves Western North American bats by rousing them from hibernation and wasting calories they don't have. Providing fruit flies with food choices can shorten their lifespan. When milkweed is scarce, monarch caterpillars are more likely to headbutt each other out of the way. Southern sea otters are at increased risk of heart disease when their diet contains high levels of domoic acid, a neurotoxin produced by warm-water algal blooms. When extreme rain events lower the salinity of their habitats, coastal dolphins can contract "freshwater skin disease," leading to lesions across up to 70 percent of their bodies. White-tailed deer fawns with higher cortisol levels in their saliva have lower survival rates independent of predation levels. Bar-headed geese can hyperventilate at seven times their normoxic resting rate without passing out. Thick-billed murre fledglings sometimes hurl themselves off cliff nests and into the sea before they're fully able to fly.

How to Debate as
a Fish

There may be times in life when you find yourself trapped in the Realm of Assumptions. When confronted with those inhabiting this space, positing, *oh, you are this, thus must be that*, one thing you can do is to declare that you are a fish, and therefore cannot be pigeonholed, for you are a fish, and have no need to reside in abodes designed for birds. This response will likely elicit some bafflement, some befuddlement, during which you can seize the opportunity to wriggle away, being slippery, being a fish, and gain your freedom to remain undefinable, like many a fish, yet to be identified.

There will be those in the Realm of Assumptions who make it their mission to corner and containerize you. They will cast their net of arguments, attempting to barrelize and demoralize. *Look here. Clearly you are not a fish, for a fish is scale-based and streamlined and cold-blooded, and clearly you are none of those things and thus and must be something else instead, so come now, enough of this foolishness.* An appropriate fish-based response depends on your capacity to engage and your willingness to play along. Adopting a hearty fish stance like a mola mola means that you simply absorb any slights, shrugging off burdens like parasites and coming off none the worse for wear. Taking a fiery fish stance may help you explode off like a bluefin tuna but at the peril of burning yourself out. But since you are reading this, you are likely a contentious fish, slightly sly and outcast, relishing the chance to get bogged down in semantics, also known as the mudskipper majoring in rhetoric stance. Not all of us have scales, you may retort, channeling the spirit of the wels catfish, the manta ray, and the moray eel. Not all of us are streamlined, you might state, miming the boxy geometries of those in the cowfish and scorpionfish families. And of course the opah would have heaps to say about the whole endothermy affair, as you vouch, if she was not cruising along some outer Hawaiian shore, which is incidentally what I would much rather be doing now, so if you will excuse me, as you seize this second opportunity to escape, exit stage left.

*

The downside to engagement, any engagement, is that if it fails to shake off your assumer, it can have the opposite effect of energizing them. They may even reverse your claim of fishhood in order to discount you. *Such a shame, to be a fish, to be trapped forever underwater and know no joys, swimming round and round in the dreariest of existences.* Luckily, these are easy enough points to refute without compromising your position. Suppose I was a red-lipped batfish, you could say, who enjoys leisurely strolls along reef edges? What if I was an epaulette shark, you could argue, addicted to trekking from one rock pool to the next? From this you can even pivot into an offensive position to throw your opponent off-balance. Did it ever occur to you that I could be a tropical flying fish, holder of the world record for water-to-air soaring? Or that you are actually in the presence of an artist and architect extraordinaire, a white-spotted pufferfish about to commence construction on yet another sand sculpture, as featured on the megahit documentary series *Life Story* on BBC One?

*

But it may come to be that this expenditure of proof is all for naught, that the other party is simply arguing in bad faith or indulging in a game of devil's advocate (which, by the way, is a very silly thing to do, as if the lord of the underworld would ever need representation from a regular Joe, having assuredly access to a vast and seasoned legal team). They might needle you on personal elements you have been intentionally nebulous about—*What kind of fish? How come a fish? Why now a fish?*—all in an attempt to drop you into the confines of their mental aquarium, to seal you away behind walls they deem immutable and immaculate, unshakable and sacrosanct.

If you are not yet weary of the exchange, one tactic to break their position and their box is to appeal to authority, which is usually a logical fallacy, but in this case, it is acceptable because you are a savvy fish, wise to being baited and keen to do some baiting in return. Plus this salvo stems directly from the good word of Dr. Seuss, well-respected and world-renowned. Point to page three in his fish-based bestseller that needs no introduction for examples of fish-based outliers, including "the one with a little star" and also "the one with a little car." See page eight for more examples of those who like to "run for fun in the hot, hot sun." And note how fish can come in all fashion and forms, in an assortment of colors and number of limbs, from red and blue to two and four and six or more, answering to no one's who, what, when, or why.

There is a chance that your adversary will refuse to recognize Theodor S. Geisel's credentials. Fear not. You can escalate the appeal to higher authorities, like the College of Physicians in

Paris and their faculty of divinity, who in the seventeenth century declared the trustable beaver to be a perfect fish, fit for consumption during Lent. Or you can cite the statute established three centuries prior, when King Edward II created the designation of "Royal Fish" to encompass whales (and porpoises in a subsequent clause) within three miles of the British coast, deeming them so superior in their fishy qualities as to deserve the Crown's esteem. For more recent rulings, point to the precedence of bumblebees in California being ruled as fish under the state's endangered species act, and thus being granted equal protection under the law as the neighboring Shasta crawfish and salamanders, with both normally lying outside of standard piscine convention. More than likely this mix of papal decree, royal edict, and binding legislation encompassing furry fish and blubbery fish and flower-loving fish will supplicate even the most fiendish clients and their representatives, who will hopefully, finally, leave you in peace.

*

This last section is for those unlucky enough to be cornered by those still insistent on the rightness of their realities, clinging so even as the day wanes and the sun sets. *But the science! Listen to the science!* These remaining individuals might be shouting into your face by this point, having abandoned all pretense of politeness and civility. *You cannot seriously continue to reason that you are a fish when you are clearly not of their lineage, not of their ancestry, not of their blood!*

Faced with this kind of reaction, you can, should you wish, pull them aside and away from onlookers and passersby to disclose a previous conversation you had with a former cladist, who confessed after a similarly exhausting exchange that the term "fish" is in reality quite a useless classification these days. Any clade that contains all fish must by definition also contain those who are not fish, thus making the whole exercise taxonomically futile. Either we are all fish or none of us are fish. Faced with this predicament, you have decided to cheerfully champion the former notion, to fully embrace being rather than not.

At this, your opponent should be thoroughly disoriented by this revelation, and he may ask you why—why go to all this length and insist on belonging to a group that means everything and nothing? To this you can shrug and also ask why—why go to all these lengths and not simply let another live, to afford them the kindness and dignity to define themselves and not be subjected to an order not of their making?

Hopefully, as your adversary ponders over your response, daylight will have faded and night will have fallen. All this stalling should have provided the chance for the two of you to be alone. At this juncture, you can, should you wish, complete the encounter by inflating your mouth like a gulper eel, or unhinging your jaw like a barbeled dragonfish, or stretching your stomach out like a black swallower, or doing whatever you need to do as a yet-to-be-discovered abyssal abomination to gobble up the unsuspecting goose, which incidentally tastes much like the cladist, so equally obsessed with the arrangement of their little Realm of Assumptions, equally oblivious as to how they had gotten themselves into this pretty kettle of you-know-what, or never grasping that for some, there are ways besides words to win a debate.

Giving Up on
Your Dreams

Sometimes things in life just don't pan out, like if all you wanted to do growing up was to fly, but fate saw fit to furnish you with bad eyes, plus a dose of red-green color blindness, the sum of which can disqualify you from becoming a pilot. Grounded by such shortcomings, you may find yourself commiserating with the ratites, a motley clan of birds that includes the emu, the kiwi, the cassowary, and others, most of whom are born without a keel bone to hang their aerial ambitions. Unlike them, you can still be cleared for takeoff; all that is required is a statement attesting to your ability to soundly operate an aircraft. But this workaround would still be a diminishment of sorts, since you would not be permitted to fly commercially or at night, when the cockpit buttons conspire with runaway lights to overtax your visual circuitry. Perhaps this is a subtle way for life to say some dreams are not meant to be. Besides, you wouldn't want to end up like the tinamou, the lone exception to the otherwise flightless group of ratites, the only one endowed with a sufficient breastbone but without much of a tail to serve as rudder, so that when the poor bird is frightened into flight—which is not an activity anyone wants to be startled into—it might steer its partridge-shaped body into objects sometimes stationary, sometimes fatally—which is not an outcome anyone wants to think about while aloft—and maybe this is another way for life to say some dreams, even if technically achievable, should remain unfulfilled.

*

At times you might find yourself teeming with many dreams but without strong inclinations toward any of them. One solution is to hedge your bets. Place your many eggs into many baskets and see what springs forth, as amphibians do with their jellied prospects while they live between worlds. You could get lucky. Up might hop a red-eyed tree frog and talent agency seeking photogenic clients! Up might slither a slender salamander partner of the most gregarious nature! But most likely nothing will arise and never will, for the majority of hopes fostered yet untended are swallowed up by opportunists lurking in the reeds, or swept out to ill ends, or left to desiccate on forlorn shores. In such circumstances it might prove wiser to abandon the scattershot approach and run with one ambition, all the way up onto solid ground, where things are less chancy. This is what the amniotes did in the post-Carboniferous age, investing in eggs that were also sturdy baskets so that each aspiration could be harbored in some semblance of safety. Whether the shells were rubbery or hardened or internalized depended on their respective reptilian, avian, or mammalian manufacturer (there is some wiggle room in this, what with green anacondas live-birthing dozens of miniature clones, and lactating mother echidnas laying dime-sized leathery orbs), but the important takeaway is that each egg contains within all the necessary ingredients for dream reconstitution—think of a dried soup mix made with love but better: no need to add water. Packaged thus, an amniote's potential can be realized anywhere—beneath shifting desert sands, up high on crags and aeries, in a skillet shimmering with oil (sometimes egg musings lead to omelet cravings)—anywhere you, fellow amniote, deem fit.

*

While diving headlong into a grand dream can be a praiseworthy endeavor, it may be wise to exercise some forethought before plunging too deeply into any single pursuit. For passion can often descend into obsession, and specialization can lead to a narrowing of aperture and the exclusion of so many things that make life delectable. Take dinner. To be able to range on spoiled mangos one moment and rattlesnake heads the next; to raze a row of cherry tomatoes before crunching on ticks found during after-dinner grooming—the gastronomic flexibility granted to the Virginia opossum is lost on those dedicated to the school of myrmecophagy, or the exclusive consumption of ants and termites. Surprisingly students of this discipline are legion; anteaters from South America and pangolins from Africa; numbats and those aforementioned echidnas from Australia. Rarely have mammals of such different stripes been so united on any single cause. Yet subsisting on an insect stipend day in and day out can become a tedious affair. Even the occasional formic-acid-filled fire ant, with their bitter citrus notes, will not do much to brighten up the taste of so much pulp and grub and dirt. (Though the act of breaking and entering into a termite fortress might itself inject some spice and variety.) By the time one commits wholly to trading in their jawline for a tube snout with mucous tongue, it may be too late to back out of this winnowed course of life. The southern tamandua may never again snack on camu-camu fruits ripening on the riverside trees they clamber upon, not having the dentition to partake in these sour treats. Nor can the aardwolf ever gnaw on wildebeest ribs with its spotted hyena cousins, lacking the metabolism to subdue anything larger than a breath mint. And while there are graduates-in-training who break with tradition—like the sloth bear, who sneaks the occasional jackfruit sprinkled with mowha tree petals and a generous helping of honey (the restrictions are fuzzier on insect-produced foods) into its buggy diet, or the aardvark, who uses its secret teeth to dine on secret underground cucumbers, digging into the earth in search of these watery gourds and in so doing becoming the cucurbit's sole pollinator—these are exceptions to the core tenet that unites this dietary discipline. What I am trying to say, dear reader, is that there is nothing wrong with wedding yourself wholly to a vocation. Simply realize that monomania carries opportunity costs, as many a silky anteater might attest to after the fact.

*

And sometimes to realize a dream demands the courage to walk away from another. Or to wade away, as was the case with *Indohyus* during the early Eocene, back when the Indian subcontinent was busy crashing into Asia and wrinkling up the Himalayas. Tired of being harassed by eagles for trying to make an honest herbivorous living, *Indohyus* the mouse-deer-pig took refuge in water and discovered a penchant for sinking, thanks to its dense hippo-like leg bones. Like a tech hobbyist tinkering in their parents' garage in the 1980s, *Indohyus* likely had no idea that indulging in its favorite pastime would lead to one of the greatest success stories in history, pivoting subsequent generations away from the landlocked grind to become blue ocean strategists. The transition from *Indohyus* to true whales took less than ten million years, which in geologic time is the equivalent of a snack break or the meteoric ascent of one tech giant if measured in modern business cycles. As success begot more success, *Indohyus* descendants spent less time hiding in forests and more time basking by the Tethys shallows in what is now Northern Pakistan. Once the roadmap was clear, the shift from land to sea was made wholesale—terrestrial ventures be damned—no hedging bets, no chickening out, although some mission statements were dropped along the way as protowhales shifted from pious herbivory to carnivorous debauchery in their commitment to the one true vision. Over the eons, the lineage came to roll out one iconic iteration after another, ranging from *Ambulocetus*, which excelled at filling the furry crocodile niche, to monstrous *Basilosaurus*, which ruled the seas with its bone-crushing bite, to the kinder, gentler ocean-sieving giants we know and love today, like Big Blue Baleen, a member of the Mysticetes, which, if rumors are true, might place Aristotle in even higher esteem, for the name might have originated from his phrase, *(ho) mūs to kētos*, translated as "(the) whale (called) the mouse," perhaps a prescient nod to one little *Indohyus*, who chose to take the plunge into new possibilities long ago.

*

Thus the trick of chasing the right dream seems to lie in knowing when to chance and when to forfeit, for pursing something so nebulous so fiercely can often cloud one's judgment and make one lose sight of the end goal. The yellow underwing moth makes the mistake of ruining itself upon candle flame not through an innate love of heat but by conflating it with heaven's light by which it steers its life's course. What is it we truly seek when we dream of flying? If it is freedom, then this prevalent desire may prove to be an unexpected trap, as the aforementioned ratites have discovered, at least on an energetics level. Laughing at gravity for any length of time is a tiring business, not so much in the face but more in the constant flapping, which necessitates a regular intake of bugs or fish or sticks of butter, the latter of which would be ideal in caloric density but are difficult to procure in the wild. Thus the question must be asked: Why fly under your own power when you can fly coach? Or: Why fly under your own power if you don't have to fly at all? The latter was the crux of the matter for ratites, who chose to abandon their aerial affairs on no less than five separate occasions to instead partake in simple earthly delights, such as shuffling along in green spaces and dining at leisure on grassy forage. Being released from having to feed the metabolic furnace has been a great boon and also constitutes a different form of freedom. Perhaps this grounding strategy was how ratites managed to carve out niches across the world, dwelling long on island Edens, at least until humans arrived to muck things up, twisting dreams into nightmares for the elephant bird of Madagascar and the giant moa of Aotearoa, the fates of both must be mourned another time—may God rest their flightless, feathered souls.

*

Perhaps prescience in dream-chasing also comes down to self-knowledge. By rejecting the expectations imposed by others, you can devote time and effort toward what truly works for you, such as growing stout and taking up track and field. Such was the case for the Somali ostrich, sturdiest of all living birds. Not needing to train his pecs for flying means that every day becomes leg day, as the ostrich might disclose during one of his rare, nonditzy moments, when he isn't showing off his dressy ruffled feathers and blue-hued gams, or boasting his half-marathon time against any four-legged creature under the African sun. When pressed for secrets on his life philosophy, he may choose to respond in his own peculiar way, by unsquiggling his rubberneck to stare through you with billiard ball–sized eyes before suddenly bouncing off like a shot, like a blur. Thus you will receive a living reminder that dreams are not only ends to aspire toward but acts to be embodied, and here one does, with a heart thrice your size, with verve loaded into each two-toed, tendon-taut step. Exercising the right dream to its fullest extent can encompass one's whole body, one's whole being, one's entire life. And it can be complete. And it can be enough.

*

But not for all. Maybe it is in the nature of dreams and dreamers to be inexplicable, to shift and reform around unforeseen currents. At least this proves the case for most of us made of swappable cells, who must constantly replace our organic parts. At what point will we have changed so much as to no longer be the sum of our former iterations and associated ambitions? You could turn to ancient Greek philosophers and their dusty warships for insight on this metaphysical conundrum, but better yet may be to query those practiced at donning and shedding selves new and old over the course of their lives, like certain members of the *Anguillidae* family. The European eel is among the few to practice catadromy, which is simply a fancy way to say backward Pacific salmon living (this is when a young fry would travel from its provincial streams out to the ocean for some flashy living before returning home to spend its final days to spawn). *Anguilla anguilla* embraces the opposite path, instead beginning in the Sargasso Sea as something resembling nothing like what it will one day become, so leaflike and see-through and strange that even Aristotle was stumped when quizzed on an eel's origins, shrugging that it must spawn from the wet guts of the earth (even the wisest of us is not always right, and that is a comforting thought). It took until the twentieth century to discover that eel larvae hitchhike for a year or three along the Gulf Stream before devoting their lives to the goal many aspire toward: securing prime waterfront real estate in the European countryside. Morphing into their familiar sinuous shapes but retaining their transparent nature, glassy eels ball together and wriggle resolutely up waterways, even if it means writhing out of the water and over one another, across paddocks and up rock walls, all in order to reach a peaceable pond. Once there, they will spend their prime years becoming yellow but never mellow, devouring anything they can cram into their mouths until, one day, a more serene vision beckons, after which they will circle back to the brine from which we all arose and shall in the end return. Once this choice is made, the eels take on a silver sheen. They stop eating and their stomachs waste away. They become beautiful and more keenly eel than they have ever been. Thus anointed, these piscine prophets depart as mysteriously as they arrived, and even after two thousand years of scrutiny, we still do not exactly know where beneath the Sargassum they go to meet their maker. Perhaps in this final phase, eels no longer dream but instead become dreams, transforming into as yet an unclassified form, harnessing a lifetime's prowess in slipping away to elude that final curtain call. We do not know. All we can see is that armed with a clarity of vision and faith, the eels flow down the rivers and out to sea, dissolving into those fathomless depths that lie beyond sight, beyond thought, even while the sun above rises and sets, the world spins, a mote chancing across space.

Going Down to
Ground

If icebergs were floatier, like mandarin ducks or sweetgum trees, perhaps the RMS *Titanic* would still be sitting in dry dock, happily rusting away after decades of ferrying ostrich feathers and dragon's blood and first-class fat cats in Turkish baths, coasting on its untested reputation of being nigh unsinkable. But alas, freshly calved icebergs are more like hippopotamuses with freshly birthed calves, both nine-tenths surface-shy and bottom-heavy in the drink, both lethal to wayward ships and their unsuspecting crews. Some might regard such territorial assertions as overreactions, but both parties merely seem to value self-sovereignty more than most. Perhaps icebergs and hippos foster disdain for up-close face time because they do not wish attention directed toward their secret philanthropy. Antarctic icebergs act as mobile oases in the desert that is the Southern Ocean, stirring up water columns and releasing land-locked minerals to various marine denizens. Ugandan hippos serve as amphibious nutrient pumps, grazing grasses and forbs by night, fertilizing stretches of river with dung and silica by day. Respecting the borders of these submersible entities is a win-win policy, as it allows them to continue contributing to the greater good on the down-low, much to the glee of bristle worms swirling beneath the ice, much to the delight of guppies brunching on half-eaten greens, and definitively to the relief of deckhands and boat hulls that remain unbucked and unbuckled everywhere.

*

Few in this world possess an iceberg's lofty albedo or a hippo's blood-sweat sunblock (which is neither blood nor sweat—think of it more as a stink lacquer) to ward off the bright light of scrutiny. To hide from prominence, the mole cricket employs the shovel claws from its mole-like front half to burrow into the dirt and provide shelter to its bug-like back half. The similarly reclusive but unrelated star-nosed mole can also be regarded similarly, in segments: mole in the back is followed by mole in the middle is followed by mole head tipped with a multi-tendriled nose that is smaller than a fingertip but six times more sensitive, able to process what is grub and what is grit in less time than it takes for you to blink. Then there is the American shrew mole, not to be confused with the Chinese mole shrew, not to be confused with the Australian marsupial mole (which comes in northern and southern varieties) or the African mole rat (which comes in furred and naked variants), all of whom have gone full fossorial to eke out existences out of the limelight. Adopting an underground lifestyle comes with perks and trade-offs. One can fully realize their architectural ambitions as long as natural lighting is not part of their design philosophy. Shelter from spying eyes is a win for privacy advocates but comes at the cost of rendering one's own eyes beady and obsolete. And the soil's free climate control and thermal buffering advantages? Benefits granted only to those willing to entertain cave-ins and claustrophobia as lifelong companions.

Luckily, the social elements of subterranean life need not hinge on soil-based existential threats. One can be as solitary as members at Talpids, Desmans, and Co., wholly obsessed with tunnel-extension plans and earthworm procurement, or one can be as communal as black-tailed prairie dogs, chit-chit-chattering within coteries within wards within entire towns underfoot, complete with nurseries and granaries and domed mounds upon which to situate sophisticated sentry systems. And while the adage "if you build it they will come" is generally true, one need not be an ecosystem engineer to enjoy the vibrant underground scene—merely being acquainted with a competent constructor will do. Meerkats are happy to occupy the burrows of cape ground squirrels rather than excavating their own, cohabiting easily with the original craft-rodents alongside springhares and highveld gerbils. Collared anteaters and collared peccaries in the Pantanals have been photographed coming and going from resting holes scythed out by giant armadillos. And southern hairy-nosed wombats dig and abandon so many burrows across their territories that rock wallabies, brush-tailed bettongs, and even fairy penguins frequent them as timeshares. Squatting without permission is not without risk, as more than one opportunist has learned after stumbling into warrens still occupied by their architects. One moment the fox's brain deems there space to slink past the napping wombat to snatch up her baby joey; another moment the fox's skull is crushed between the cavern roof and the wombat's raised backside of fused bone and muscle—hopefully, mercifully, far too quick to register much regret at rousing the mama builder and bulldozer.

*

Despite cave-ins and heave-outs, many continue to take the deep dive down, forsaking blue yonders and bruised sunsets to slip below forever. This impulse might be easier to understand from those who do not possess eyes. The Japanese daikon, the Cantonese lobak, and the Korean Joseon radish are content to drill their cylindrical taproots through compacted ground, cracking channels for water and nutrients to penetrate even the densest hardpan, and so saving the part-time gardener from having to rototill their weekend vegetable beds. The shepherd's tree ranging across the Kalahari and Namibian Deserts can plumb nine-tenths the depth a giant sequoia towers skyward in height, dousing to find the same groundwater that deep-drilling rigs nowadays seek. Through this delving, the shepherd's tree has inadvertently become a local symbol of hope, providing shade to overheating rhinoceroses, nourishment for starving giraffes, a coffee substitute for those in need of a pick-me-up, and a hemorrhoid herbal for those who would like to sit back down. By following their inner drives for deeper delving, both radish and tree have become the most uplifting and stomach-able forms of saviors—the accidental, incidental kinds, doing by not doing, helping by being present, serving through self-sustenance.

*

Of course, one need not be blind or plant to understand the pleasures of being enveloped by the world. Surrendering to warmth and darkness is the innermost desire of many a house cat on YouTube, as documented through the presentment of many a cardboard box to prospective felines. Flatfishes of the sea, like Scottish folds on the web, are also creatures of comfort, favoring hiding spots from which they can watch the world without being spied upon in return. The butter sole, the scale-eye plaice, and the arrowtooth flounder have gone all in to reorient their lives toward the dual acts of hunkering down and looking up, migrating their left eyes to the right sides of their faces (brills and turbots do the opposite, being staunch antidextrists), pattern-matching their top halves with their surroundings while perfecting their undulation choreography to ensure complete burial into sandy bottoms within seconds. This hide 'n' bide approach is excellent for ambushing unsuspecting minnows and guarding their cream-colored bellies against ospreys, but it has proven ineffective against those operating without eyesight or oversight, like benthic trawlers guided by equal parts of ignorance and appetite, removing fish and substrate and coral colonies in less time than it takes to say, "Super scrapers scour sea life from the seafloor."

*

Faced with forces beyond our reckoning, many of us continue going to ground, as if the habit has also entrenched itself into our beings. As the light grows wan and the ice seal-scarce, the pregnant polar bear carves a den into snowdrifts and riverbanks in preparation for the tiny miracles swelling within. When the river changes from murky water to baked mud under a withering sun, the West African lungfish chews into the earth to entomb itself inside a mucous cocoon. Tired of a world of weirding weather, some reptilian brains default in doing, tasking their respective lizard or snake or turtle operators to find a nearby hole and gear down like an old clockwork. Perhaps these acts of privation are necessary for moderating lives lived in extremes, through times wavering between light and darkness, at interludes buffering present and possibility. Maybe these rituals of retreat are instructive in helping us muster the resolve we need to face an increasingly volatile world, to surface answers to questions we have not yet grown wise enough to ask. Could the late storyteller Barry Lopez have intuited correctly, as he did on so many occasions, that quiescence is requisite for enacting the arctic dream? What if lungfish estivation is essential to lungfish rejuvenation, a prayer to wash away the self-forged prisons made of mucus and inner turmoil? And what does the marginated tortoise ruminate over more during her bouts in deep brumation—her peaceable life lived thus far or the uncertain days to come?

Maybe we as a species are missing something vital by never knowing what it's like to go dormant for a spell the way sessile oaks and fat-tailed lemurs do. Consider the latter, nine-tenths us in genes, grafted onto our present-day civilization. For three to seven months each year, eight billion lemurs, gorged with fruit and flower nectar, would log out of their lemur virtual meetings and shut down their lemur straw factories to curl up inside their arboreal apartments. Lemur power plants would shut down. Lemur wheat fields would lie fallow. Geopolitical tensions and autocratic ambitions would cool off during this bout of torpor, with everyone seeing the beautiful prose over the revenge messaging woven into that most famous of lemur plays, penned by that most renowned of lemur bards: *To sleep, perchance to dream, aye-aye, 'tis no rub at all.*

I wonder if humans in turn would be content with such a swap, to live tail-sufficient among Madagascan baobabs and flame trees. Would our ambitions lead us back down to the ground, back on our roads of striving and world wroughting? Perhaps. But perhaps through such a species exchange program we can come to experience other ways of being that will take hold in our psyches. Lemurs may learn to look, *really look*, up at the stars, while we humans may learn to pause, *really pause*, to see the roots of creation; and together we might trace the path from the common womb whence we both emerged to the common clay where we shall one day both return, singing the praises of an earth that has long sustained our mortal coils, this dark and wild country, which remains, to this day, the only place to craft the primate soul.

6. Rebound

The diabolical ironclad beetle can survive being run over by a Toyota Camry—twice. Young alligators are able to regenerate their tails up to three-quarters of a foot. The denuded *Geckolepis megalepis* looks like a raw chicken tender but can regrow its shed scales in a few weeks without scarring. Increased beaver populations in the Cascade Range are reputed to raise the reproductive rates of northwestern salamanders. The population of North Chinese leopards in the Loess Plateau is increasing due to a government five-year reforestation plan. In Fukushima, returning wild boars roam the inner excluded zone's abandoned streets while Japanese serows stick to outer human-inhabited areas, possibly to avoid the boars; macaques prefer the in-between areas. Thick-billed murre fathers can feed fledglings on the open seas twice as often as both parents can feed chicks still nesting up on cliffs. The East Pacific red octopus appears resilient to heightened levels of ocean acidity, given five weeks to acclimate. American pikas cope with rising temperatures by retreating to underground taluses during the day. Coral reefs in the Eastern Tropical Pacific are more heat-resistant than reefs in the Caribbean and the Indo-Pacific, possibly due to an ecological memory. "The key to survival for future reefs may not be an immunity to stress, but rather an ability to recover and regrow after stress," notes ecology professor James W. Porter.

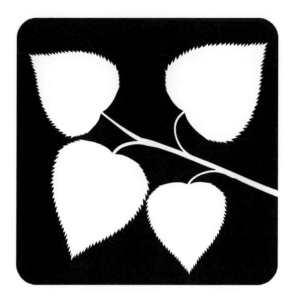

Creature Career
Counseling

Are you trying to find your new niche in a reconfiguring world? Do you feel less than content at work, wondering if there is something more? If you are reading this in between act and act, take a moment to reflect on life, even as life inflects around you. Perhaps a consultation with your colleagues at Tree of Life Inc. will prove insightful, especially if you can arrange a meeting with some of the senior partners. They may be willing to disclose qualities that helped them compile their extensive curriculum vitae, helping you to strike a new path forward or, at the very least, help you find the courage to make a virtue out of your own singular, evolving peculiarities.

*

Frustrated by ineffective management at work? Consider taking a sabbatical to go sailing awhile with siphonophores and their associated subsidiaries. You may recognize these colonial organisms from their oceanic ventures of renown, such as the appropriately christened *Praya dubia*, reputedly one of the longest creatures in the world, or the Portuguese man o' war, reputedly one of the most venomous creatures in the world. Siphonophore division of labor policies mean that everyone who joins has a vital role to play within the larger organization; specialized positions exist in a variety of departments to match any temperament or aptitude: siphon and gas bladder maintenance through Transportation (Job Code: PNEUMATOPHORE);

point defense and harpooning duties with Mergers and Acquisitions (DACTYLZOOID); enzyme biochemistry and nutrient processing via Digestion and Extraction (GASTROZOOID); or gene shuffling and medusa replication in Mass Manufacturing (GONOZOOID). Regardless of the position you choose, job satisfaction is guaranteed, for pointless drudgery is what dulls the heart, and aboard a colonial organism, there is no meaningless work. Helping the greater whole sail along the wind's whim; ensuring that everyone is fed the sea's finest; depending on others and being relied upon in return—for many there could be no better fit or fate. But a warning before enlisting to serve in this seemingly utopian enterprise: the genetic fine print of the contract is binding. Vertical movement is limited, with little opportunity for advancement. Signing up means being set both for life and for good. But the travel perks are grand.

*

Should becoming a lifelong cog for a mindless, faceless predatory conglomerate fill you with familiarity or dread, consider work that instead champions more worthy causes. Whether you are a fledgling fresh to the injustices that abound, or a bone-weary veteran who has been fighting the good fight for decades, learn the art of sustaining your inner drive without burning out by taking a scenic drive to south-central Utah. There, at the Fish Lake National Forest on the edge of the Colorado Plateau, watch for the glimmer of golden leaves on the windless morn. Below that spot will likely be where PANDO the aspen giant resides, dispensing counsel to those who heed the call for service. The key to supplying the world with hope, according to the trembling hundred-acre guru, is to practice regular self-care, to bury yourself in the earth so that your chief clonal mass is buffeted against the ravages of frost and fire, against recurrent cycles of grief and despair. Only when you are grounded thus can you do the work you were meant to do and for the duration it needs to be done, whether that be until the next fiscal quarter or through the entire late Pleistocene, eighty thousand years on. Only then, PANDO persists, can you ensure your community of tender starts will take root and flourish, speaking and swaying as one to spark the change you so envision.

*

Maybe you are one who resists conformity of any type, yearning to chase the paths and schemes you long harbored within. If this is the case, then a freelancer's life may prove an ideal fit. But be forewarned: being the master of your own fate is not for the faint of heart. No aid from friends or family shall ease you through nights made sleepless by portents of failure, by the hard knowledge that the world at large holds little reprieve for the solitary spirit. Here is where consulting creatures with singular lineages may afford you fortitude, for each will have a tale to tell about rising to the occasion even as others faltered, having learned the hard art of going at it alone.

Consider the duck-billed platypus and her viral marketability, on being able to leverage her chimeric persona to generate impressions through controversy and adorability. Learn not to cross the line like the mountain beaver did, who in trying to reposition himself from his paddle-tailed celebrity cousin, veered into eccentric territory and became a fern-eating recluse. Even if your sui generis branding isn't quite on point like the pronghorn's, who to this day is still mislabeled as a mere goat or antelope, take heart and continue to put in the legwork of establishing a keen vision like the pronghorn does, whether it be through steely vigilance so you can spot wily coyotes encroaching on your turf, or through sheer agility so you can outpace your competition so successfully that they become obsolete, as the fleet-footed ungulate did against the North American cheetah division.

Playing to your strengths is one key to freelance success. Consider targeting a specific market like the aardvark does, catering its skill set almost exclusively toward reaching the termite demographic. Being pigheaded can help you break down any potential barriers that keep you from accessing new stores of prospective clientele, while being thick-hided can shield you from the jeers of all the heckling hyenas gleeful to see you fail. For criticism will come your way regardless of the choices you make, so stay strong and heed the cautionary tale of the pen-tailed tree shrew, who, in coming close but failing in its audition to become part of the main primate lineage, resorted to soothing its woes with near bodyweight amounts of fermented nectar from the bertam palm. Such behavior naturally draws a crowd, attracted by the shrew's talent to drink but not get drunk; but sadly there is now no longer a way to distinguish the former performer from the mask it wears and masquerades behind.

Perhaps the best piece of advice for a prospective freelancer is to shore up the borders between one's personal and professional life. Consider studying awhile under the tutelage of the walrus, an Odobenidae original and a master of shrugging indifference, whether it be to the frosty reception of its arctic environment, or against the desperate nips of polar bear pretenders, or even by the occasional tusking from members of its own tribe. The walrus simply abides, accepts that everything is just business in the vying for shares of shore and accolade. There are never any hard feelings as long as payment continues to come in clams, and even if there are, the whiskered pinniped is too blubber-coated to show any signs.

*

Perhaps after years and decades of toiling toward and for, you find yourself seeking a more radical change in your life. Instead of turning over various permutations of work, maybe what you really crave is to drop the definition altogether. So if conventional ideas of career success have worn you down, if workplace rules and politics have soured your soul, if you are seeking a path out from the crushing grind, then turn once more for guidance from those in the more-than-human world. Embark on a road trip to the roughest and wildest country of your choosing. There, on the bark of the scraggiest pine, by the scree beneath the tallest cliff, on the broken piece of shale next to the heel of your boot, you may find the answer you are seeking. For housed there, within each splotch of paint or frill of leaves or nest of thread, is a lichen enterprise, each a master class of communal living, with two or three or even more fungal, algal, and yeasty entities mining soil meanings out of bedrock together. Here, at the edge of the frontier, beyond the noise and norms of external expectations, something new blooms from the very old. Devote a day or two or a lifetime here so you have sufficient space to watch and be; for among one of the many delicate lessons imparted by the way of the lichen is that there is seldom any hurry to anything once you have found what you have long sought—such peace, this joy, a belonging.

Reinvention Is a Matter
of Necessity

The moorland hawker nymph refashions himself late in life, much like Ebenezer Scrooge. After terrorizing his less fortunate neighbors for years on end, he will rouse one morning and shed his entire way of being, also like Ebenezer Scrooge. Unlike Dickens's famous miser, we are not privy to the spiritual visitations responsible for the nymph's sudden change of heart. We can only surmise that his spectral trio is unlikely to apparate on Christmas Eve—what with ponds generally being frozen over and all—and that they may manifest as visages of the insect's life stages: the Egg of the Past, the Naiad of Now, the Imago to Come. Whatever the impetus, the nymph will proceed to emerge from his underwater home, clamp onto a nearby reed, and commence the last of his dozen molts. For once, he will not simply cure into a larger iteration of himself with a more nightmarish set of extendible jaws but become a wholly reconstituted being, complete with compound vision and a compound name that suits his new persona: dragonfly. This nascent reborn—also termed a teneral—will proceed to dedicate his remaining weeks to fulfill a new life purpose. But unlike Scrooge or the birch borer or the checkered-skipper, the metamorphosis a moorland hawker undergoes is incomplete. Dragonflies and damselflies can change their forms but not their souls, perhaps because they do not undergo a pupal stage and thus do not still themselves long enough to ponder upon their past transgressions. Instead of being the bully bug beneath the pond, the moorland hawker merely becomes the bully bug skimming above it, gorging himself on as many mosquitos as he can catch, harrying females of his kind so aggressively they are forced to feign death, clinging to his boorish traits until the hour the moment the wintering world clamps down, claims him.

*

True transformation takes genuine commitment. Should you one day decide to shed your landlocked life to become a child of the sea, heed not the advice proffered by skipjack tunas or king mackerels or any who seem to paint underwater living as an effortless dalliance—they likely have had the privilege of furrowing through fluid and little else. Instead, take note of those coming from more diverse walks of life, those who once scrambled over rocks or soared on overhead, only to veer from their expected trajectories to embrace something novel. The gentoo penguin sacrificed much to achieve hydrodynamic mastery, forsaking her wing beats for flipper sculls to outdive her cormorant competitors; now she glides through the seas with the grace her ancestors could only achieve streaking across the sky. In comparison, the northern sea otter and the southern fur seal remain works in progress when it comes to securing aquatic carte blanche; both still sport fur coats and ear tufts, traits long shed by the harbor seal (a true seal) and the harbor porpoise (a true porpoise), respective blubber brothers from distinctly different mothers. But perhaps the ones that strove the hardest and came the closest to achieving their marine ambitions were members of the Ichthyosaur order. After the worst mass extinction the world has ever known, ichthyosaur ancestors made a fresh start in the emptied post-Permian seas. But forging an

aquatic livelihood from scratch is a tall order, even for the most skilled terrestrial national. Imagine being in possession of a vintage Fire-Breathing Fortress LEGO set (lucky you) and given the instructions to build the Black Seas Barracuda (also another classic set). Inevitably, your improvised pirate ship will contain bits of dragon wing, chunks of castle turret—though some of the treasure chests may be laterally transferrable. This is similar to what ichthyosaur ancestors had to do, converting reptilian building blocks into aquatic apparatuses, like rigging a bottom fin out of a kinked tailbone or sculpting the top fin out of nothing but soft tissue and cartilage. All things considered, they were remarkably successful in their ventures. *Ichthyosaurus* itself outsharked the sharks of its time in shape and speed, thrumming across the ancient seas two hundred million years before the Greeks ever entertained the slightest portent of dolphins. The fossilized *Shastasaurus* found at Lilstock seemed to be as gargantuan as any modern-day whale-based leviathan. Then there was *Ophthalmosaurus*, apt to delve down to where the light scarcely penetrates, scouting twilight waters with eyes the size of soccer balls, possibly in search of the only other animal endowed with such ocular majesty—a colossal squid with peepers the size of dinner plates, or at least their Jurassic ancestral equivalent.

*

Drastic changes in lifestyle can be a long-labored process; there is no need to reinvent the wheel all in one go. Perhaps it would be helpful to eschew wheels for describing this transformation altogether, like nature has seemingly done over the arc of its history. For while there might be some tumbleweeds out there, some roly-polies to be sure, and many a dung beetle that have devoted their lives toward the art of spherical architecture, biologists have yet to come across any radial-tired roadrunners, any tread-fitted tarantulas, no matter how efficient these configurations may appear on paper. This might be because wheels by their nature insist on all-or-nothing perfection: square wheels and lumpy wheels and never-ever-wheels are all equivalent in their uselessness for locomotion. This binary mandate of wheel forms lies in stark contrast to the diversity of crab forms, which includes a spectrum of stout, serviceable designs, all graded good enough for swimming or scuttling or whatever one needs to do in this ever-changing world. Members of the Decapoda order have no qualms tweaking the base body plan to suit their needs, having gone back to the drawing board on multiple occasions. To be crab-like is to be amenable to being malleable; it matters not whether your lineage be true (clan *Brachyuran)* or false (clan *Anomura*), so long as you follow the core tenet to shrink your abdomen and broaden your cephalothorax. One is free to be conservative and go half-crab, like common squat lobsters still overfond of their tucked tails, or to push beyond convention and become knobby-peared stilt-walkers, like Japanese spider crabs. Gaudy-clown or yeti-haired, flower-moon or teddy-beared, even red-and-white and polka-dotted: whatever you and your niche deem crab enough is good enough. Versatility. Adaptability. Well-roundedness. These are the traits that have come to define crabs across lagoons and around deep-sea vents, in freshwater brooks and up coconut trees, and these are the traits that can come to define the new you, so long as you don't let perfection stop you from taking that first step.

*

Maybe it is helpful to imagine the path toward reinvention less as a yellow brick road one is warned never to stray from (*beware those flying monkeys!*) and more as a rainbow road of possibility, with branching trails all embarkable given the right timing and circumstance (*yes, flying monkeys and . . . ?*). Life itself has taken this approach to many a literal heart. Distinct from the rust and red pumping inside you and me, the blood of a giant key-hole limpet runs true blue, being copper-based. The green tree skink bleeds a shade somewhere between lime and jade, while hues of purple-violet course through lamp shells and peanut worms. Then there is the ocellated icefish, sporting antifreeze proteins instead of blood cells, rendering its insides as clear as the surrounding Antarctic waters. Across eras and phyla, a host of hemes and means have tackled the chief task of fer-rying oxygen throughout the body, demonstrating that wildly differing solutions can converge on the one true way, so long as the purpose is common and the cause paramount. The Koh Tao Island caecilian and the European glass lizard may not dwell in the same class or even the same continent, but their mutual love for burrowing pushed them both to go legless and limb-free. Then there are the night-loving bats and water-loving belugas, two groups united only by their poor eyesight and love for in-cessant chatter, somehow coming to cultivate similar brands of echolocation with which to parse their disparate worlds.

*

With such a multitude of options going forward, you may find yourself at a crossroads without proper guidance. What is important then is seeking that inner clarity. What is *your* concrete vision of better? Future you could be equipped with more of your existing strengths. If you pride yourself on being self-sufficient, consider the path to become C4 photosynthetic, like plants from nineteen families have independently done. Should you delight in being stimulating around company, strive toward being positively electric, as fishes from six distinct lineages have evolved to become. What is important then is leveraging those existing assets. C4 corn and C4 daisies and C4 grasses repurposed their metabolic pathways to develop a more efficient means of making sugar while wasting less water. Electric eels and rays converted their twitch muscle cells into voltaic piles to dazzle even the most cynical of audiences. Of course, future you could choose to go the opposite route, deciding instead to shore up any present shortcomings. Consider dedicating yourself toward eating healthier and cultivating a broader palate, like sundews and bladderworts did on nine separate occasions by adopting bug-based diets to address their nitrogen deficiencies. The Australian pitcher plant even crafted in-house solutions for its venture into carnivory, modifying its leaves into pitfall traps for unsuspecting flies, repurposing fungal-fighting enzymes for digesting curious ants. Knowing what you want. Using what you have. Becoming more than you are. These are sure and sound tips for devising a newer and better self.

*

All this talk of reinvention may prove overwhelming, prompting you to withdraw and shut down. It is only natural. How nice it might seem to live simple and single-celled like bacteria found off the west coast of Australia, to go unchanged in habit and form for two billion years! But chances are you do not dwell in a deep-sea sulfur environment and have no real wish to be locked in stasis. Chances are you prefer to change as the world does, sometimes subtly, sometimes seismically. Maybe you are secretly thrilled at being startled by flamingos taking sudden flight, or watching shaggy troupes of musk-oxen assembling in semicircle formations, even should such encounters come a-charging into your peaceable days, and life becomes stranger and scarier than you care to admit. For there is some genuine peril at having things go awry, some justified fear: the price for leaping into the unknown and falling can be steep. Even during the halcyon days of the Cambrian half a billion years back, when radical realization was the norm and the seas roiled with revolutions of body and mind, failure proved far more the rule than the exception. Sporting five eyes and a vacuum-hose snout, the experiment that was *Opabinia* spawned no modern descendants of any kind. *Anomalocaris*, with its eyes on stalks and a camera-shutter mouth, fared longer but not much better, lasting into the Ordovician before being supplanted by fish fare, albeit the jawless variety. And no amount of hallucinogens could help one conceive of a follow-up to *Hallucigenia*, a creature so bizarre that scientists once reconstructed it upside down and backward, mistaking its spines for its legs and its front for its end. Throughout the ages countless forays into the new availed not despite much availing, with there being little to show for things save a few impressions left on shale, a resin cast or two on museum shelves, some traces barely recollected at best, with most lost, forgotten to time.

*

The weary and jaded might wield this to claim that there is nothing new under the sun, that everything has been tried and trialed, so better stay with something proven and sound, like being an accountant or an actuary, or settling on neutral paint tones like accessible beige or agreeable gray. Yet if each life is not a chance taken, an hour of bold choosing, for what reason are we born? Besides, any actuary worth their salt will know that to live is to risk, that every action entails it, must indeed, with each of us granted a finite set of years before our bodies become forfeit. So while it may be that we fail in our attempts to truly transform ourselves, we shall have at least braved trying to be more than we are; and maybe, just maybe, if our luck runs true and our hunches pay off, we can find ourselves buoyed by the same fortunes that bore *Pikaia gracilens* to grace, that diminutive Cambrian upstart that went on to give rise to all vertebrate life, and so supplied this otherwise muted world with resplendent quetzals and rainbow boas and troupes of all-too-clever apes, some bold enough to don coats of many colors as they serenade, others left to daydream on beaches of crabs in idiom and reverie, *pensando en la inmortalidad del cangrejo.*

7. Sustain

Prairie lupine was the first plant to regrow on the Pumice Plains by Mount St. Helens after the eruption in 1980; the purple perennial fixed nitrogen from the air while burrowing gophers and wandering elks aerated the ash. A community of life unknown to science was observed around deep-sea hydrothermal vents at the Galápagos Rift in 1977; one study site was named "Rose Garden" because the tube worm inhabitants had red tips and resembled long-stemmed bouquets. Leafcutter ants have been cultivating fungal varietals across rainforests and grasslands for sixty million years. Ambrosia beetles, along with ants and humans and certain termites, also practice a form of agriculture. Returning in 2002, researchers found that "Rose Garden" had been wiped out by a new lava flow. Subsequent exploration revealed a new vent field nearby, colonized by a juvenile assemblage of tube worms, mussels, and clams. The site was christened "Rosebud."

Pick-A-Mix,
Build-A-Beast

In the heyday craze of Beanie Babies and megamalls came the notion that one could stroll into a shop and walk out with a perfect companion. Such a concept, to design a friend to exact specifications! Maybe a classic teddy bear with a home-sweet-home shirt and white sparkle flats. Maybe a promise puppy with a squeeze-to-play tune and bubblegum scent. But with mallrat culture and in-person retail falling out of favor these days, it is proving trickier to access these craft-a-creature services, or at least the stuffing machines with vortex technology necessary to achieve optimal polyfiber distribution. Perhaps this is for the best. Too much candy and cotton filling can become tiresome. Do spring frogs and *Triceratops*, famed for their elusiveness and suspected for their orneriness, need to be reduced to a base snuggleability factor? What if, in this post-heyday age of ours, people are craving something less avatar-like and more freely animated? Perhaps solace for the soul is found not in an escape to the safe and franchiseable, but rather in the embrace of the wild and remnant, the stranger-than-fiction, the yet-to-be-known. If this sentiment piques your interest, here is a guide for discovering a being you may know but never knew you needed; an instructable for imagining a creature you've never heard of but will be eager to encounter; a manual for populating your inner sanctum with inhabitants nonplussed and nonplastic, guaranteed to prosper long in the mind.

*

Step one: Close your eyes. Begin the build-a-beast journey in your head, at the head. Choose from a variety of facial adornments—brows, bumps, horns. Two and bushy: a Snares penguin, with eye-catching crests running down to the base of the bill. Five and bony: a Rothschild giraffe, tipped with ossicones, those highly held head bumps that are odd in number and arrangement. Feeling weirdly nosey? How about a whitemargin unicornfish, sporting what is politely called a "rostral protuberance," developed during its awkward larval phase?

Utility can factor into your selection process. Horns, for example, can be used to ward, to warn, or to defuse otherwise costly conflicts. Most lions, living and nonliving, know or knew that the cape buffalo can either gore them with the tips of its horns or deliver blunt force trauma through its "boss," a name appropriately given to the mass of fused bone over the bovine's skull. Then there are the black-and-orange spines on a hickory horned devil, useful in deterring hungry birds from snacking on the hot dog–sized caterpillar. And one glance at the helm curl on a dominant bighorn sheep conveys everything younger challengers need to know: don't waste my time or your energy on a bout you have no chance winning.

Puncturing, playacting, peacekeeping: there is likely a horn for every whim (or in the case of the unicornfish, horns even without conceivable causes). The material itself may be immaterial, for a horn can be bone draped with velvet, which is technically antler and seasonal in nature; or the horn can be chitin and lifelong for jousting, like the one sported by male Hercules beetles, sprouted from their thoraxes. Sometimes horn can even be tooth, like the oversized, spiralized canines mounted to the fronts of most male and some female narwhals. Pushing through arctic waters with a ten-foot enamel-free tooth might seem like a nightmare to anyone with receding gums and ice cream cravings, but for these sausage-shaped whales, such sensitivity may be another way to gauge their surroundings. Scientists theorize that the organ, shot through with millions of tiny holes and nerve endings, may be capable of detecting minute changes in salinity or chemicals released by prospective mates. A horn can thus even be a sensor, a mood checker, a tool for unlocking an otherwise imperceptible world.

*

Step two: Select a desired covering for your beast. Take your time, for skin is not only accoutrement but also integument, essential for the integrity of self. Look past the faux fuzz, the polyester, the velveteen—a suite of natural options has been time-tested for fit and function. Consider going beyond the standard hair and feather options, varied as they are. Consider scales, so underrated by most mammals except for pangolins and musky rat-kangaroos but widely embraced by a host of other groups. For delicate styling sensibilities, the glitter attire of butterflies and moths may prove ideal. Nanostructures on each microscopic scale papering each wafer-thin wing offer chemical-free coloration, built-in iridescence, even a degree of dust and dirt protection. This latter quality is especially relevant for sphinx moths and southern darts, petite speed junkies with no access to wing maintenance postmetamorphosis; and also to material engineers seeking inspiration for the next generation of self-cleaning fabrics. Imagine marinara sauce lifting right off those starched linens! Envision chili oil beading from your crunchy sequined top! What a world it would be to devour with abandon, to dive bib-free into every Manwich platter and variation of vindaloo!

Looking for something more substantial? Consider reptilian scales. Moisture loss was a key consideration in the development of their line of waxy keratin-reinforced epidermis, which also boasts UV protection. This tough waterproof coating comes with options for every occasion. Simplified elegance in action? Slip into something from the snakeskin series and test-drive five forms of limbless locomotion—sidewinding is a particular hoot—made possible through an optimal friction balance between belly scales and ground surface. Interested in interactive facades? Chameleon skin pebbled with chromatophores provides the perfect canvas for showcasing emotional states in real time. Going into hostile territory? Don scutes as necessary, like many an alligator or turtle—each additional bony plate under the skin provides additional coverage against those looking for a fight or a snack. Naturally, fashion need not be sacrificed for function. The San Francisco garter snake, the dwarf day gecko, and the ornate diamondback terrapin sport just three of the many dazzling color schemes in the reptilian catalog. But be sure to check on availability, especially for those three; quantities are dwindling, and no restocks are anticipated in the foreseeable future.

Should your tastes be more inclined toward streamlined classic chic, it's hard not to go fish. Placoid, cycloid, ganoid, ctenoid—a gamut of scaling choice exists for every niche. Interested in low-maintenance performance wear? Look no further than sharks and how they cover everything with a layer of dermal denticles—slip-smooth one way, sandpaper the other, and so easy-peasy slimming that sharkskin-inspired swimsuits were banned at the Olympics for giving athletes an unfair advantage. Want to go full Renaissance fair instead? Consider a set of arapaima armor, scale mail that is laminated, mineralized, and evolved to resist against all forms of blunt and piercing trauma. (It's even rated against piranha bites, should you ever feel the urge to go for a swim in the Amazonian basin during the dry season, when the water gets a bit too low and company a bit too chummy.) If grace in motion is your overriding consideration, spend awhile perusing the salmonid palettes. Each fish in the family acts as its own curator and fashion model, from the silver-shifting-to-crimson bodies of spawning sockeyes to the prismatic dazzle of rainbow trout spawning their namesakes. Some serious anglers swear by Dolly Varden chars returning from the sea in a striking orange polka-dot number with dark-olive backing. Others are more beholden to the starry reds and yellows of certain coaster brook trout, who spend their lives in crystal-clear streams. Here might be an instance where deciding on which is best is moot, for all are designs so sublime that even the late author and nonprofessional fisherman Cormac McCarthy chose to end his Pulitzer-winning novel with trout, describing their sleek, burnished bodies as patterns beyond all reckoning, as maps and mazes to the world in its glory and making.

*

Satisfied with your choice of headdress and outfit? Continue onto appendages and accessories. Starter tetrapod templates are available for those who wish to limit their options to four limbs or less. Even within this constraint, the range of choices is considerable. For a limb can be a propper-upper, a digger-dugger, or a cherry-picker. Four matchstick legs on tippy toenails can shoulder a metric ton of Shire horse. Spade-like nubs on the hind legs of Mexican burrowing toads help them retreat into their empire of dirt. The hand on a tufted capuchin is capable of four power grips and at least sixteen precision ones, probably because opening tucum nuts with stone hammers requires more technique than strength. A limb can be a terror, a carver of earth, a render of flesh. Giant anteaters rip open termite mounds by hooking in their scythe-like claws and pulling their arm toward their bodies. Harpy eagles snatch nutcracking monkeys with talons that can envelop a human fist. Limbs working together can form a symphony in motion, working in concert to shepherd their bearers across land, sea, and air. Young Cuban crocodiles can gear-shift to an ancestral gait when they feel the urge to gallop. California sea lions can pirouette at forces of up to five Gs with the aid of their oversized flippers. Rufous hummingbirds can scull the skies with buzz-strokes of figure eights, both to hover in place and to fly the two thousand-plus miles between the Rocky Mountains and the Mexican state of Guerrero. Limbs need not be literal wings to serve as figurative wings of desire, just as their bearers need not fall from grace like the angels featured in Wim Wenders's film also titled *Wings of Desire*. But if six-limbed arrangements do pique your interest, consider broadening your world to include insects. (This is a good exercise to do in general.) Four legs for day-to-day clambering onto branches plus two arms for once-in-a-while clamping onto mates work well for the wandering violin mantis. Or go further with cephalopods and bump the digit count to eight arms in giant Pacific octopuses, to ninety cirri in the chambered nautilus. (A tip: Suckers come standard on most tentacle models, but hooked and barbed attachments on said suckers are more commonly featured in squids.)

For the appendage-adventurous, feel free to stretch the limits of what limbs can be and do. The common sea star can taste while trotting with its water vascular system, tipped with hundreds of tube feet on each of its arms. Opt for sheer volume by plumbing the depths of Western Australian mines for *Eumillipes persephone*, the world's only millipede to live up to its moniker of a thousand legs, as confirmed in a thrice-count by a blurry-eyed entomologist. Scientists suspect the millipede is driven less by an obsession to find the underworld queen that forms its scientific name and more by a craving for fungus that fuels its molting process, which helps to create more legs, which in turn facilitates more burrowing, and on and on it goes, a miniature bulldozer set on top of a wave of mostly limbs.

*

Now armed (and legged) with these steps, you too can summon a myriad of creatures to mind at will. Random combinations are fun when you do not know what you are seeking and wish to be surprised. One horn plus bumpy skin plus odd-numbered toes may net you an Indian rhinoceros. (Dial down the size a tad and get a male Javan rhino relative.) Two horns plus reptile scales plus no legs can land you a Saharan horned viper. (Or tweak the horns to three and limbs to four and get a male Jackson's chameleon.) No horns, scales, or limbs? No worries: hagfish are always set as a default, although their prodigious slime production and uncomfortably loose skin make them tricky to embrace or stomach. The key to satisfying conjuration is to be imaginative but not too imaginative. For we have yet to discover a five-horned, ten-limbed, color shifter (although a Caribbean reef octopus mimicking a piece of coral comes close), plus this is not a guide for building chimeras or plants—the former group contains too many heads to be viable, while the latter contains too many variables to be permutated. Besides, there is currently no demand for a grow-a-plant manual so as long as the chief way remains the easiest and most popular: sow-a-seed, do-a-dance, say-a-prayer.

*

At the end of an official Build-A-Bear™ experience, an official Build-A-Bear™ employee will also ask you to do a dance before picking out a heart to place inside your creation. Inserting the mass-produced plaid or satin heart inside the almost complete plushie is a symbolic gesture—unless you want a real sounding ticker, which costs extra. Of course, for your custom creation process, you can forgo fabric hearts and sound-chip hearts and even oxygenating hearts altogether, citing reasons of tackiness, expense, or general pointlessness. Hearts are not essential in many creature clades, and not having one doesn't render any of them less tender. If anything, the reverse may be true: many of the world's most heartless are also among the world's most forgiving. (But beware of overgeneralization: some sponges are coarse-glass-gritty while some corals are sting-trigger-happy.) There are advantages to forgoing matters of the heart. No need to guard your insides from the outside if you can acquiesce to the sea's will like a Deepstaria jellyfish. No need to bother with the whole circulation business if you can be as thin as a Persian carpet flatworm. (Considering a last-minute color

swap? Peruse the marine flatworm collection for fresh ideas.)
And why risk heartbreak from mingling when you can go solo
in doubling like a starburst anemone, budding off a piece of self
to build another you?

Maybe such notions of presence and absence and cloning are
beside the point. What are we talking about when we talk about
heart? As it may prove to be for coral polyps and tube sponges,
the heart we obsess over in so many of our stories and sagas is
not a mere pump or knot of muscle, but rather a core essence
from which some cadence of being arises, thrums of ongoings
that comprise the fierce living on this planet, this rock—itself
a larger venture in the shaping of patterns into a strand of music
three-plus billion years in the making, played out against the
backdrop of an older community that may or may not be lis-
tening, a universal commonwealth from which Mystery with
a capital *M* resides, even as it rises and falls to its own incalcu-
lable rhythm—all of which are very much beyond the scope of
this guide.

So You Want to Write an Animal Essay

Well, so do I, and after writing a book of them, I feel like it is time to set out some ground rules. Since writing a regular essay requires one to know the regular parts of speech, writing an animal essay—so goes my thinking—surely requires one to become versed in animal articles. Of which there might be eight, or eight hundred. I do not know. I am not an animal grammarian or even a regular grammarian. I come across sentences and creatures these days like everyone else, by futzing about on the internet, by skimming Grammarly and *Australian Geographic*. But things are getting a bit chaotic in the mind palace. Close to bursting. And since revisiting seems to be how regular essayists orient their way through regular essays, here is an attempt to craft an animal essay in real time by going back to the bones. Cartilage? Some sort of building block. This is all a work in progress.

*

Nouns seem like a solid place to start. Everyone knows nouns as everyone is a noun. Without nouns things would be less than ether, less than thought, a bygone nothing—all of which are ironically nouns. Nouns can be abstract, or nouns can be sound, but nouns can never be sounds-like—those would be adjectives. Animal nouns of the collective variety seem to be popular these days. People love to luxuriate in owl parliaments and rattle-snake rhumbas, in the unkindness of ravens and the murders of crows. But don't sleep on the solitary animal noun, lovely and lithe. *Ocelot. Caracal.* It might seem like I am just naming cats. *Margay. Serval.* Which is not untrue. But I am also trying to demonstrate the power a lone noun can have, perched up on a tree or lurking in savannah grass, muscles taut for ambushing a fellow noun, preferably of the rat or warbler variety. *Puma!* This doubles as an interjection—so consider that checked off the list. *Jaguarundi!* This is less emphatic, there being less cat, but if someone hollered this, you would still want to turn around, for jaguarundis are very shy and awfully pretty.

*

Maybe one day you will grow tired of speaking nouns, nouns like *lumpsucker*, although I cannot imagine why, with lumpsuckers being so adhesive and adorable. But this may be a good time to segue into pronouns, which can step in as substitutes. Consider if you have a lunch meeting at noon but also wish to list all the parasitoid wasps in existence, of which there are more than beetles and will take you more than a morning to spell out the half-million-plus members of this most speciose of groups. Here a simple "they" can save your weekends and sleep schedule, "they" being suitable for all sorts of abbreviations and applications, plural or singular. The latter I confirmed with the *Merriam-Webster* people, as they kindly awarded it their "Dictionary Word of the Year" in 2019, probably for being so accommodating. Feel free to use it liberally to address anything from entire orders of aphids and lacewings to a single recently realized butterfly, should they make such a request of you. This seems to save everyone's time, while being the right and respectful thing to do.

*

Of course, nouns and pronouns without verbs are at best potential and at worst taxidermied, primed to gather dust inside glass cases forever. Sentences without verbs are robbed of their sentence identities, just as animals can find themselves bereft without their animal habits. What is a baby goat without its gamboling? What is a male greater sage-grouse without his lekking? A stilled hummingbird is a mere feathered puff without the thrum of its name, and without swimming, many a shark can go as far as to drown, which is technically still a shark behavior but a rather temporary and tragic one. Of course there are those keen to embrace their static verbiages, like sea vases and Venus's flower baskets. Both seem fine at being occurred to by currents of happenstance, maybe because external turbulence is all they can stomach without possessing actual stomachs. Likewise, the slender sea pen is a passive feeder that has no objections to being described in a passive voice, shying away from the center of attention in any sentence, content to remain in its states of flow and simple being.

Still other animals like to don their verbs while mixing and matching their actions to their characters. The cock crows as the wolf hounds while the rabbit quails. Several in the mustelid family relish the opportunity to doppelgang themselves as both object and action, being mischievous. The ferret ferrets while the weasel weasels as the badger badgers. One can get skunked by a skunk and stink, which is fun to say but unfun to experience, for it takes many gallon cans of tomato juice to fill a bathtub (which doesn't even work; try peroxide instead) and ten days for the skunk to restore its odorizing talent, rendering it temporarily garbage-scented and thus delectable. While otters can't yet otter and martens can't yet marten (or maybe they can, but only the late author of the novel *Marten Martin*, Brian Doyle, would know), I can see it happening in the near future, maybe taking the form of a barrel roll, or some sort of stomp 'n' romp, followed by a slip 'n' slide into dark waters. Then there are mustelids that prove resistant to being double-featured: a surprising no to the fisher fishering, choosing to dine on land porcupines instead of porcupinefish; a definite no to the wolverine wolverining, being too stout (but not stoat, which in turn is not quite weasel). Perhaps the latter, being the largest member of the family, already has all the twin-naming it can handle, still sore from being saddled with the Latin name of *gulo gulo* (meaning glutton glutton), miffed at being associated with both a deadly sin and a personality flaw.

*

Adjectives. Mark Twain and Stephen King have said that they should be used sparingly, like spices to accent a balanced meal with nouns as nutrition and verbs as regular movement (they most likely did not say the latter, but I am writing this before dinner and am reading between the lines). But sometimes you might crave pecans, candied and caramelized, cinnamoned and cayenned, especially while in the midst of figuring out how to adjectivize and alliterate a bevy of assorted animals. The trick to this—it turns out after refueling with some mixed nuts—is to add the suffix *-ine* to the end of their Latinized monikers. *Lupine. Ovine. Asinine.* These are excellent for regular use, for who does not vacillate between feeling wolfish and sheepish and braindead stupid over the course of a blood sugar roller-coaster ride? But consider heightening your sentences even more with fresher creature descriptors. *Bombycine. Hippocampine. Hystricine.* For all you know, a dash of silkworm or seahorse or old-world porcupine (crested or caped—chef's choice) might be exactly what your subject stew of an essay needs.

It is at this point where Hemingway the app, and most definitely the ghost, will rise up to admonish you, warning you about the perils of adjective-induced highs, urging you to pare down on the adverb usage. But it is your right to be as weak-verby and flourish-fancy as you please, so long as it truly and honestly reflects your intentions and is not done willy-nilly or out of timid thinking. I'm sure the adverbs themselves would be pleased, having been crammed away and discouraged from use by the authorities for so long, and just because someone somewhere used them lazily, unthinkingly. So go forth and find your own voice and be as doggedly and battily and owlishly as you desire; but maybe not carpingly, because no one likes being known as petty or fussy in faultfinding, like that judgmental fish who shamed the aforementioned wolverine for having poor table manners.

*

Beyond the big five comes the need for a refresher. Sure, I can read how "prepositions relate words to other words and aid in syntactical context," but working through examples is the best way to get concepts to stick. The star pearlfish hides *inside* the sea cucumber's anus. The tongue-eating louse swaps *in* for the spotted rose snapper's ex-organ. After eight weeks the botfly emerges *from under* the skin of its human host. Prepositions are helpful in figuring out where things go and in what order, like who is host and who is parasite. It is important for both parties to be clear in their roles as to avoid confusion, for it would not make sense for a robin to sneak its eggs into the nest of a common cuckoo, nor for you to cling to the insides of a beef tapeworm, for the latter is flat and ribbony and you might not have a scolex for attaching onto. (This image is useful in highlighting both sentence and scenario with dangling prepositions, and thus making everything easier to assimilate.)

*

Next come conjunctions, the bond runes and mortar words upon which to set meaningful connections and phrases. Some people prefer only to think in "either" and "or." Maybe their world is simpler that way, less scary to think about. Either a fish is fish-stickable or it is not. Either a bird is oven-roastable or it is not. But such uninspired conjunctive usage may lead to punctuated worldviews, ill-suited for a planet teeming with "ands" and "fors" and "whatevers." Since Antarctic krill, thus Adélie penguins and crabeater seals and southern fulmars and fin whales (this is grammatically suspect but trophically sound). Rather than only cod-collapsible-cod, the sea also stocks argentines and silversides, snakeblennies and porbeagles, grenadiers and alewives (part-time), saris and sculpins, and so on and so forth, up and down along the water column, all of them hopelessly dependent. This makes the whole exercise problematic on a sentence-building level but delightful on a world-building one, especially if one desires their home to be linked and lively and thriving.

*

And I do. The more I write, the more I realize I am less interested in the mechanisms of an animal essay and more in figuring out how to manage this growing menagerie. Of course, to maintain a menagerie, one should really know how to manage a conservatory, and if I have to do both, I might as well embrace the whole lot. So comes the end of this venture in essaying, I'm afraid: I'm off to puzzle over the grammar of plants, to do some conversing with water, maybe a session of vocal training with wind, maybe a round or two of mineral studies. This will take all the time I have I suspect, what with all the wildly differing rules and syntaxes for each tongue, if they can be called that. Maybe this is why the earth took so long to get its act together and look convincing. If you have stayed until now, hoping to gain insight on writing an animal essay, I'm afraid this might come as a bit of a disappointment. Apologies. You could try instead studying the works of the aforementioned Doyle, himself the author of "The Greatest Nature Essay Ever," himself also a lover of run-on and grammatically suspect sentences. But should you also wish to establish your own inner safari, which in Swahili just means "journey," you are welcome to any of the findings I have gleaned since beginning this endeavor. Tips like mixing wordplay with earthplay. Tips like switching views and shifting senses. Go outside and spend some time by a riverbank at dusk, maybe in the autumn light. Note the skein of geese overhead tracing a haphazard V. Hear the sound an acorn makes falling from the oak leaning over the shore. Note how it differs from the plop of a minnow breaching the water surface. Stay with the ripples that never entirely subside. The adjective for twilight is *crepuscular*. A word or tome may exist for the feeling of silt slipping between your ring and middle finger. Use whatever tricks you have to remember. *Linger.* Recall this moment and all that was present. *Witness.* Bring it back whenever you need, whenever you can. *Crane.*

Brief Thoughts on Almost Every Mentioned, Mostly Living Thing (in Alphabetical Order)

Aardvark	Always first in listings, like those businesses that begin with "AAA" in phone books, when they were still a thing.
Aardvark cucumber	The only plant that has managed to persuade an aardvark to eat its vegetables.
Aardwolf	Fell far from the hyena family tree. Awkward at gatherings and reunions.
Adélie penguin	Smaller than an elephant. Tuxedo trim and white eye-rings complete the "scared to go to prom" look.
African elephant	Larger than a penguin. You know what an elephant looks like. If not, you are in for a treat!
African golden cat	Comes in pretty much every color and pattern except gold. The equivalent of calling a cat you don't know *Kitty*.
African mole rat	So much more to this group besides the naked variety. Some are blind, while some headbang to greet one another.
African puff adder	Wikipedia entry: "These snakes do well in captivity, but gluttony has been reported." Relatable.
Alewives	Technically, the singular fish is called an alewife, but they seem keen to keep in groups.
Alligator snapping turtle	Keep fingers, broom handles, and pineapples away from the beaked business end.
Alpine swift	All swifts can be alpine swifts if they soar high enough.
Ambrosia beetle	Actually a weevil, but all weevils are beetles, so this is technically accurate. Is named for what it likes to eat (a fungus), not what it tastes like (god nectar).

Ambulocetus	Mostly snout and teeth and fur. Not as cute as an otter.
American alligator	Mostly snout and teeth and scutes. Just as cute as a crocodile.
American badger	*Badger badger badger mushroom! Oooh it's a snake! Badger badger badger* . . . This will only mean something to those versed in early 2000s internet memes.
American bison	Humpy. But all muscle underneath, unlike camel humps, which are all flab and fat. Or so I've been told.
American robin	Orange chest. Blue eggs. Apparently literate in color theory.
American shrew mole	Called a shrew because of the fur. Called a mole because of its teeth. But what it really resembles is a pocket gopher.
Ammonite	Formerly known as snakestones in medieval England. Now the title of a romantic drama starring Kate Winslet. Fame whisks one to strange places.
Andrews' beaked whale	Deep-sea squid slurpers. That's about all we know.
Andriashev's spicular-spiny pimpled lumpsucker	As round and knobby as one would expect. Comes with an adhesive disc. Good for accessorizing rocks.
Anna's hummingbird	Most Annas would be thrilled to have one, but alas, hummingbirds are filled with too much sugar and wanderlust to be kept in a cage.
Anomalocaris	Previously classified as a jellyfish, then an ancient sea cucumber relative. Now its name means "abnormal shrimp." Paleontologists tried their best.
Antarctic krill	One of around four hundred trillion. Enough for every Anna out there should they want a consolation pet.

Antipodean albatross	Probably a corresponding bird exists on the opposite side of the world. Probably based around France.
Aphid	Sapsucker. The plant equivalent of a mosquito but worse, what with plants not being able to scratch.
Arapaima	Skittish for a big fish. Steer clear to avoid getting slapped by two hundred pounds of muscle.
Argentine	Just a silver smelt trying to make its way in a big blue sea. No regional affiliation, despite the name.
Arnoux's beaked whale	Prefers to stay down deep but is forced to come up for air. Like a mountain hermit in inclination but reversed in elevation.
Arrowtooth flounder	Two nouns and a verb mashed together to form a fish. Not the cause of its mushy meat—that comes from a parasite.
Asparagus fern	Probably doesn't make your pee smell funny but still not a good thing to eat.
Atlantic cod	Not related to black cod, blue cod, rock cod, or ling cod. Not a very close-knit family, the cods.
Atlantic salmon	Can return to the ocean after spawning. This anticlimactic trait makes it less popular for leading roles in nature docs compared to its Pacific cousins.
Australian marsupial mole	Prefers burrowing through lightly cemented sands, not the loose stuff—that's coarse and rough and gets everywhere.
Australian pitcher plant	Also called the Albany pitcher plant, which seems like a galaxy far, far away from its native Jarrah forests of Southwest Australia. But distance means less when you can't move.
Australian tree fern	A mole that's not really a mole. A pitcher plant more related to apples than other pitchers. Now a fern that can grow up to fifty feet tall. All perfectly on-brand for being Australian.
Axolotl	Yes, very cute. But can it frown when it's sad? If not, the smile doesn't mean quite as much, does it?

Aye-aye	Taps on tree trunks to find bugs to eat. Think a furry woodpecker but instead of a beak, long skeleton-esque middle fingers.
Banded archerfish	Capable of recognizing human faces. Would they spit their waterjets at those they like or hate?
Baobab tree	They don't call it the "tree of life" for nothing. For many, a world entire.
Barbeled dragonfish	Makes light instead of fire like a standard dragon. The giant fangs are the same though.
Bar-headed goose	Seems to prefer the head-on approach when it comes to dealing with obstacles, even if they are the Himalayas.
Basilosaurus	People who are worried about *Megalodon* still being alive should worry more about *Basilosaurus* still being alive. Which it isn't. So don't worry.
Basking shark	Described as lazy and lethargic. But try weighing four tonnes and swimming with your mouth wide open. That takes effort.
Beaver	Seen as competent and industrious. Learned long ago not to open their mouths while swimming and working.
Beef tapeworm	Live abroad. See the world. Settle down in a cozy host and raise one hundred thousand offspring. Can't fault its life philosophy.
Beluga	High up on the chatty whale scale. Cute chirps and whistles to us. Calls of doom for schools of smelt and herring.
Bertam palm	Boasting the booziest of nectars, fermenting to a respectable 4 percent ethanol content.
Bhutan glory	What a name for one to live up to. Doesn't seem to faze the caterpillars in their first six months of life.
Bighorn sheep	*Size–feature–thing*: Usually a tried-and-true naming strategy, but this one comes across as a tad bland and obvious.

Birch borer	Technically, it's the bronze birch borer, but the alliteration got to be a bit much.
Black marsh turtle	Not a basker, which is a bit of an oddity among turtles. Also the constant smiling. Very suspicious.
Black swallower	Banned at most all-you-can-eat establishments due to sporting an expandable stomach.
Black vulture	The all-black plumage suits the bald head. The spread-wing stance and the grunt-hissing completes the punk aesthetic.
Black-tailed prairie dog	Favorite food of the black-footed ferret. Only food of the black-footed ferret. Bit of a risky venture, to be so picky.
Bladderwort	Branding needs work for this whole group of amazing plants.
Blue sheep	Is it? Maybe in a certain light, if you squint.
Blue whale	Yes, yes, very big. But maybe it should be remembered for qualities other than size. Bluish in a certain light? But that might just be the water.
Bluefin tuna	Probably wishes people would again regard it to be only good for cat food, like in the old days.
Bone-eating snot-flower worm	Someone had fun naming this. The opposite of the person in charge of naming bighorn sheep, it seems.
Bono's Joshua Tree trapdoor spider	Rushes out of its burrow to inject its prey with venom. Unclear if entomologist and namer Jason Bond was a U2 fan or hater.
Boomslang	The baby version might be in the running for cutest deadly snake, with its giant emerald eyes. Don't get bit.
Boreal chorus frog	Audible but unpindownable? A universal experience of encountering small frogs that seem both everywhere and nowhere.
Borneo camphor tree	Crown-shy, but maybe not root-shy. What happens underground stays underground.

Borneo flat-headed frog	Flatness as a quality to aspire to. Respect.
Borneo tufted ground squirrel	Literally more tail than squirrel. Maybe should instead be called the Borneo squirreled tail.
Botfly	Don't google botfly infections if you are squeamish. You won't like it.
Bottlenose dolphin	Can be jerks to sharks and porpoises.
Botulism	Archnemesis of canners everywhere. Chief culprit of the great sausage poisonings in Germany during the eighteenth and nineteenth centuries, resulting in the worst wursts.
Boxfish	Not the most appetizing shape for a fish. No one has ever had a boxfish craving.
Brachiosaurus/ Giraffatitan	The cranes of the animal world. Besides the actual cranes of the animal world. You know what I mean.
Brambling	A verb as a bird equals a finch on a beech. So one saying goes. This one.
Brazilian free-tailed bat	Designing a fast plane? Maybe model it after a bat, said no one ever. Maybe they should.
Bristle worm	The second-most beautiful group of worms. Not meant as an insult, but it can come across that way.
Bristlecone	Can get old as hills. Arguably almost more hill than tree, with wood that erodes instead of rots.
Brush-tailed bettong	One of those that never needs to drink. Teetotaler taken to the extreme.
Bumblebee	Formerly known as the humblebee. But this is a much better fit and obvious to anyone who has seen it fly.
Butter sole	The one on your plate, drizzled with that lemon-caper beurre blanc sauce, might be up to eleven years old.
C4 corn	Better in crowds and hot summers than C3 soybeans.

California sea lion	Living the dream of many a wandering surfer.
California two-spot octopus	More like the default setting is two spots, with options to make more at will.
Cantonese lobak	Also called a white carrot, a radish, or a turnip. Can be turned into a soup, a stir-fry, or a cake. A full-course capable vegetable.
Cape buffalo	What happens when a cow realizes it doesn't have to take nothing from no one. Beware the bovine uprising.
Cape cobra	Also takes no guff from anyone, except from secretary birds.
Cape ground squirrel	Call system: "bi-joo" for lesser dangers, "bi-jo" for serious dangers. When you are small and edible, most creatures fall into those two categories.
Capybara	Has what it takes to be an official rodent mascot; a certain cartoon mouse has nothing on it.
Caracal	Comes with tasseled ears. A feature that improves most cats.
Caribbean reef octopus	Can change color. Can squirt ink. Has eight limbs. Yup, it's an octopus.
Carrier snail	The most arts-and-craft inclined of snails. Would make a great scrapbooker.
Cassowary	Listen to its call with headphones on. Definitely a dinosaur.
Catfish (wels)	This version is relatively upfront and unlikely to commit identity fraud.
Cave lion	You'd think more hair would work better for an Ice Age beast. But alas, no mane.
Cave tetra	Sight seems secondary if you have a good lateral line. Light is so contingent and unreliable, if you think about it.
Chambered nautilus	Short tentacles. Terrible swimmer. Slow grower. Has somehow weathered multiple mass extinctions.

Channel Island mammoth	Weighs in at around a tonne. A mini-mammoth is still a little mammoth.
Checkered-skipper	Check-skipped out of the UK in 1976. Reintroduced back from the EU in 2019. Let's hope future reintegration efforts don't take as long.
Cheetah (American)	The puma used to have a faster, leaner buddy in North America. Now it's all by itself. Cue the Eric Carmen song.
Chimpanzee	Everyone talks about Ham, the first great ape in space. No one talks about Enos, the first chimp to orbit the earth. You did good, champ. You did good.
Chinese mole shrew	Can also be Vietnamese, Thai, and Myanmar in origin. Mixing moles in with shrews sows more confusion. Need a new word, like "shmoles."
Clouded leopard	Another pretty kitty looking for space to hunt and climb and vanish into.
Coaster brook trout	Threatened in their native range. Invasive in their introduced habitats. Poor fish just wants to live its life.
Coelacanth	Just to be clear, the individual is not four hundred million years old. Though a caught specimen did come in at an impressive eighty-four years.
Collared anteater	Enjoys, on occasion, a meal of honey with a side of bees. No stink beetles, please.
Collared peccary	Not actually a pig. Hard to wrap one's head around that, given its appearance.
Colossal squid	Not shipwrecking kraken size but still plenty beefy. Sports eyes each the size of a large pizza.
Common cuckoo	Which came first, the clock or the bird? The bird, of course. It's always the bird, getting those worms.
Common sea star	Can eat up to ten regular mussels a day. We might be able to eat more, but we probably don't savor them as much.

Common squat lobster	Despite the name, more focused on claw size than on lower body development.
Common swift	Despite the name, there is nothing ordinary about flying between Sweden and the Congo, year in, year out.
Cookie-cutter shark	You'd think it would be impossible to focus on anything else but that set of chompers, but get this—a belly that glows green.
Coral reef	We can also form reefs, but they are usually made from bones and garbage and plastic. Not as big of a tourist draw.
Cormorant	Where being a great swimmer makes you a bad flyer: a classic study in trade-offs.
Cowfish	Can come with bright polka dots or honeycomb patterns, unlike sea cows or land cows, who are drab by comparison.
Coyote	Best animal cameo in a film? Cue the coyote in Michael Mann's *Collateral*, just before "Shadow on the Sun" by Audioslave hits.
Crabeater seal	Does not, in fact, eat crabs.
Crane	Comes in wattled, whooping, white, and other varieties. The bird, not the machine.
Crazy Rasberry ant	Wikipedia entry: "Not to be confused with the longhorn crazy ant (*Paratrechina longicornis*) or the yellow crazy ant (*Anoplolepis gracilipes*)." No one would want that.
Cretan dwarf mammoth	Shetland pony-sized. As wee as a mammoth can get.
Crow, a murder of	Basically made up by a bunch of fifteenth-century white dudes trying to boast how witty they were. It's fine to just call them a flock.
Crucian carp	Sounds like Grecian 5. Now this obscure jingle from that commercial in the early 2000s, complete with saxophone solo, can haunt you too.
Cuban crocodile	More at home on land compared to other crocodiles. May also hunt in packs. Think a big, scaly wolf.

Cuttlefish	Each contains a unique cuttlebone surprise within. Collect all 120 species! Just kidding, don't do that.
Cuvier's beaked whale	Others in the collection: Cuvier's gazelle, Cuvier's bichir, Cuvier's shark (which is just a tiger shark), Cuvier's toucan (which is just a subspecies, so it might not count).
Cycad	Dino chow for the longest time. Not as popular these days, what with all the neurotoxins.
Damselfly	Not usually in distress. No rescuing required, thank you very much.
Deep-sea coffinfish	Perfecting the art of lethargy for energy conservation. Have you considered not breathing?
Deep-sea sulfur-cycling bacteria	Content to live in the same community for 1.8 billion years. Have you considered not evolving?
Deepstaria **(jellyfish)**	The original plastic bag, fully billowable and biodegradable. Also seems to support an isopod-in-residence program.
Diabolical ironclad beetle	Flight or invulnerability? This beetle made this hardest of choices when deciding on its superpower.
Diabolotherium	Named for the cave it was found in, *Casa del Diablo*, rather than for its temperament. Probably quite chill, like most sloths.
Diane's bare-hearted glass frog	This frog bears a striking resemblance to the most famous of Jim Henson's creations. That's right: Constantine, the world's number one criminal.
Dojo loach	Is sometimes susceptible to Ich. Though aren't we all?
Dolly Varden char	The story behind the name is just as folksy and Dickensian as you would expect.
Dromicosuchus	In Greek, "a fleet- or quick-walking crocodile, one who walks on stilts." Think a big, scaly wolf that's extinct.

Duck-billed platypus	The biological equivalent of hitting a cherry, a seven, and a bar on a slot machine and going, yes, let's work with that.
Dugong	A single dugong was once spotted off the Cocos Keeling Islands, presumably wanting to get away from the bustle of dugong life.
Dung beetle	Hard to make small talk with one and not touch on the work. But if you don't bring it up, it will feel weird. Hence the awkwardness at meetups.
Dyeing dart frog	More purveyor than producer of toxins, which come from ingesting specific ants, millipedes, and mites. Imagine that diet trending.
East Pacific red octopus	Maybe using color as a description isn't the best idea for a creature that can change hues at will. Size might be more helpful. This one's a small.
Eastern brown snake	Looks perpetually angry due to its raised brow bridge. Is actually perpetually angry due to being a hothead.
Eastern gray squirrel	Is probably glad it doesn't live on the same continent as eastern brown snakes.
Echidna	"A kind of sloth, about the size of a roasting pig with a proboscis two or three inches in length," described echidna illustrator George Tobin in 1792, before roasting and eating one.
Electric eel	Do not hug.
Electric ray	Wikipedia entry: "Scribonius Largus, a Roman physician, recorded the use of torpedo fish for treatment of headaches and gout." Migraine? Take two ray shocks to the temple and call me in the morning.
Elephant bird	Conversion rate is one elephant bird egg equals 160 chicken eggs. Adjust your cake recipes accordingly.
Emu	For all you history and military buffs, the Great Emu War of 1932 is essential reading.
Epaulette shark	Able to survive out of the water, making it the only portable AND portage-able shark around.

Eumillipes persephone (millipede)	No eyes, no pigments, nothing but tiny legs for days.
Euoplocephalus	Possibly the single biggest cause of broken tyrannosaur shins.
European eel	Glass. Elver. Yellow. Silver. One life-stage name is not like the other. But then none of the life stages are like the others either.
European glass lizard	Legless but not a snake. Can lay eggs or give live birth. Refuses to fit inside your boxes, unless they be dark and warm.
European hedgehog	Little spiky bug Hoovers. Much funner to watch than Roombas.
European starling	Sure, it can mimic our words, but that's just gibberish to it. Would rather chat with other starlings at the local roost, even if it sounds like gibberish to us.
European sturgeon	An ideal dinner guest. Nonfussy about presentation and will clean any plate set before it. (It may also eat the plate.)
Eyelash mite	Happy little mites. Bob Ross probably would have included them if he did portraits.
Fairy penguin	Poops out glitter made from the silver scales of fish it eats. Nature, so magical.
Familiar chat	Wikipedia entry: "a dumpy short-tailed bird 14–15 cm (5.5–5.9 in) long." The editor seems to be holding a grudge.
Fat-tailed lemur	Uses tail for fat storage. Imagine: "Oh, that's from the Thanksgiving turkey. Should last me until the Christmas ham."
Fennec fox	Big ears. Bitty body. A bona fide formula for cuteness.
Ferret	Little ears. Slinky body. Another path toward adorability.

Fin whale	A splash of white on the lower right jaw. Gray blaze patches and chevron patterns along the body. One sleek and stylish whale.
Fire ant	Fence lizards have evolved longer legs and a special shimmy just to get away from them.
Fisher	Bigger than a marten, smaller than a wolverine. For your average mustelid needs.
Florida carpenter ant	Works with wood of all types but prefers damp and rotting. Also farms aphids on the side. Truly an ant of many talents.
Flower moon crab	Do not confuse this with the Halloween moon crab. They are very different.
Freshwater sponge	Do not confuse this with freshwater algae. Also very different but even harder to distinguish than crabs.
Fritillaria delavayi **(plant)**	An example of evolution happening before our eyes; in this case, to shield itself against our eyes.
Fruit fly	Where did you come from, where did you go? Almost as annoying as the song.
Furred sponge crab	Hopefully a trendsetter. We don't wear enough hats for fashion these days.
Gaudy clown crab	One crab's attire is another's insecure critique. Wear what you want.
Gaur	Something about the monosyllables just works for bovines. Gaur. Yak. Cow. Moo.
Geckolepis megalepis **(gecko)**	Its scales can seemingly fall off at a glance. I've seen everything.
Gentoo penguin	The most distinguished of looks. That silliest of walks. A call that sounds like a clown horn. An ideal penguin to aspire toward.
Geoduck	Eventually grows too big to fit back into its shell. What an awkward day that must have been.
Giant Aldabra tortoise	Never grows too big for its shell, being welded to it. Doesn't understand the concept of a starter home.

Giant anteater	Vacuum on one end, duster on the other. There must be an anteater-themed cleaning service out there somewhere.
Giant armadillo	Call for serious termite issues. Can demolish whole mounds. Not great at cleaning up afterward though.
Giant keyhole limpet	The opening at the top is where waste is excreted. Not really a keyhole on this not really a limpet.
Giant moa	Aotearoa wasn't big enough for both them and us, it seems.
Giant Pacific octopus	This index seems cephalopod-heavy. Quite representative of the world.
Giant panda	Not the red, cute one. The other one.
Giant tube worm	Not a fan of the sun or eating. Prefers to be in the dark, absorbing.
Ginkgo tree	Rancid butter. Old gym socks. Vomit. Ah, the autumn air is again ripe with the nuanced scents of ginkgo nuts.
Golden mole	Why rely on sight when you can tremor sense? Not as rideable as the sandworms in *Dune*.
Graceful decorator crab	More refined in aesthetic than the sponge decorator crab, which specializes more in toxic-looking sponges.
Great white shark	Large, but not the biggest. White, but only the bottom half. More like mid-sized two-toned shark.
Greater sage-grouse	Named for the sagebrush it prefers to eat. Can see this being a useful approach. Tater Tots Tom. Carbonara Sandy.
Green anaconda	The chunkiest of constrictors. Beware the offers of free hugs.
Green tree skink	Who needs malaria pills? Just develop green blood that is toxic to the parasite.
Greengrocer cicada	The most neighborly descriptor for an insect ever.

Gregarious slender salamander	The most charming descriptor for an amphibian ever.
Grenadier	Be sure to specify if you mean the deep-sea fish or the soldier in charge of grenades.
Gray seal	Be sure to specify if you mean the pinniped or the Elton John song (which is not bad).
Guinea baboon	Males engage in "mutual penis diddles," which is their version of a handshake. "How are you doing today, Johnson?"
Gulf corvina	"Noise produced during Mexican fish orgies deafens dolphins." The headline writes itself.
Gulper eel	Mostly mouth but not overly keen on talking.
Hagfish	Good at knot tying and slime making. A role model for those who prefer haptic forms of learning.
Hagryphus giganteus	Picture a souped-up cassowary. The wildest colored plumage possible. It could happen. Imagination is key to jazzing up all aspects of Mesozoic life.
Hallucigenia	Three pairs of tentacles. Seven pairs of legs. A throat probably lined with teeth. Things were metal in the Cambrian.
Harbor porpoise	One average human equals roughly one average porpoise. Very size-relatable, unlike whales.
Harbor seal	Likes to lounge and nap when full of fish. A different type of relatable.
Harpy eagle	Boss in every way and knows it, which makes it even more boss.
Harvester termite	Mostly eats grass. No need to add harvester termite coverage to your policy, unless your house is made of straw.
Havtagai (**Wild Bactrian camel**)	Drinks from salty springs by the singing sands of the Lop Desert. How romantically hardcore.
Hector's beaked whale	Hopefully the last beaked whale. I've run out of things to say about them.

Helium	Flighty and noble, unlike its lighter neighbor hydrogen, which is flighty and volatile.
Hercules beetle	Is there a Xena beetle instead? Maybe a Lucy Lawless beetle. Not out of the realm of possibility, since the Angelina Jolie spider is scuttling around somewhere.
Hickory horned devil	A hungry little piggy is what it is. To be fair, it's chowing down for its future regal moth self, which doesn't eat at all.
Highveld gerbil	Cleans out the burrows every evening. A conscientious roommate.
Hippopotamus	Comes in a pygmy, less belligerent version.
Hog-nosed skunk (Humboldt)	A smaller, smellier South American cousin of the false badger.
Honey badger	A meaner, snarlier African cousin of the true badger.
Honeybee	Loved by humans and varroa mites.
Horsefly	Loved by swallows and parasitic wasps.
Howler monkey	Females must need to tune out the racket males make at some point, right?
Humboldt penguin	Sometimes found gelling with Magellanic penguins.
Humpback whale	Dating profile: Loves sardines, hates orcas. Enjoys spy hopping, bubble netting, sending custom remix tunes out for all to hear.
Humpback whale barnacles	See the world on a whale. Free food and board. Not a bad gig.
Iceberg	Little ones are called "growlers" and "bergy bits." Yes, this is official terminology from the International Ice Patrol.
Icelandic cyprine	Meet Ming the clam, dated at 507 years old. Cause of death: the process of figuring out the clam's age.

Ichthyosaurus	Not a dolphin or a dinosaur or affiliated with any group that begins with the letter *D*.
Impala	The antelope version doesn't suffer the suspension problems that plagued the sedan version. Probably why it's still in production.
Indian elephant	Like its African cousin, is also larger than a penguin.
Indian giant squirrel	A normal squirrel enlarged and run through an "enhance color" filter.
Indian rhinoceros	Strictly a browser. Prefers to sample selections, not dwell long ruminating. Bad book club member.
Indohyus	Not heavy-bottomed, just dense-boned.
Inland taipan	A triple threat of being fast, deadly, and accurate. Is also confident and doesn't feel the need to flaunt.
Irish elk	Engages in an annual exercise to test how much antler bone can be stacked on one's head before neck pain sets in.
Jackson's chameleon	Not welcomed in Hawaii. It knows what it did.
Jaguarundi	More cougar than jaguar in lineage. More otter than cat in build. A mash-up kitty.
Japanese daikon	Best vegetable cameo in a film? The Radish Spirit in Hayao Miyazaki's *Spirited Away*, sporting an upside-down sake bowl and a red *fundoshi*.
Japanese macaque	Ditched the tropics to trod through snow. Hot spring soaks probably stem some of that regret.
Japanese serow	Less cattle than goat. More antelope than deer. Sometimes mistaken for a boar. A bit fuzzy, literally and figuratively.
Japanese spider crab	Sports eight legs that are made for walking. The other two work like toy robot claws for grabbing.

Javan rhinoceros	All sixty-eight individuals can be found in Ujung Kulon National Park, next to Krakatoa. Yes, *that* Krakatoa.
Jersey Giant (chicken)	A chicken bordering on turkey territory.
Joseon Korean radish	"Jo-seon-mu! Boil them, pickle them, stick them in a soup! Lovely kimchi with a bowl of rice." So says an alternate universe Samwise Gamgee, praising another type of tuber.
K2	There is a K1, but it's overshadowed by the fourteen taller eight-thousanders.
Kalahari tree skink	Being able to live in the climate-controlled nests of the social weavers seems to be worth the noisy landlords and an occasionally peckish neighbor.
Kate Winslet beetle	Yes, there is indeed a Leo beetle, but Kate was named first.
King mackerel	Strictly a ceremonial title. Holds no authority over the Atlantic Spanish mackerel or the cero mackerel. Not even a true mackerel in ancestry.
King penguin	Thought to be the largest until the discovery of emperor penguins. Still sufficiently regal in stature to retain the title.
Kiwi	Inspiring both a nation of people and a delicious fruit. A true king of birds.
Koala	Many, many evolutionary branches away from actual bears. Though the eucalyptus obsession does weirdly parallel the panda's bamboo compulsion.
Koh Tao Island caecilian	Has no interest in scuba diving, unlike the increasing number of backpackers and tourists coming to visit its home.
Komodo dragon (pepper)	Wikipedia entry: "notable for its spice's 'delayed reaction.'" Sounds similar to an infected bite from a Komodo dragon (lizard).
Krøyer's deep-sea anglerfish	The most attractive of anglerfish. Not exactly a high bar to clear.

Kuhl's pipistrelle	Derived from an Italian word, named after a German naturalist, and can be found in North Africa. A cosmopolitan bat.
Lacewing	One of those insects you hear in passing but don't actually know and when you see it you go oh, so that's what it looks like.
Lamp shell	One of those creatures you think you know but you really don't. What is even happening inside?
Large-eared pika	Disappointing name given that they are relatives of rabbits. Far from floppers.
Leafcutter ant	Crops vegetable matter not to eat but to cultivate fungus on. Goes to great lengths not to eat their greens.
Leafy seadragon	Just a piece of seaweed in the sea. Watch how it drifts.
Least bittern	Has normal sounding calls compared to its American cousin, which sports calls resembling a loud dripping faucet.
Least tern	Prefers to sprawl out on the beach when grounded, which, to be fair, is what any of us would do after a very long flight.
Least weasel	Wikipedia entry: "The Ojibwe believed that the least weasel could kill the dreaded wendigo by rushing up its anus." Not going to top that.
Leatherback turtle	Turtle swimming champ. Holds records in speed, diving depth, and distance. Credits its jellyfish-exclusive diet.
Leopard	The middle child of big cats.
Lesser Antillean rice rat	Done in by brown rats and mongooses.
Lesser bilby	Done in by house cats and red foxes.
Lesser earless lizard	Still around and listening, even without external ear gear.
Lesser frigatebird	Gets its dinner by harassing other birds so they vomit up their catch. Gulls scrounging in garbage seem less shameless by comparison.

Lesser kudu	A little shy, a little stripy, a little threatened.
Lesser Mascarene flying fox	Another to have gone the way of the dodo on Mauritius, which included dodos.
Lesser mouse-deer	Starring role as "Sang Kancil" in a series of Indonesian and Malaysian fables. "Small yet cunning, he uses his intelligence to triumph over beings more powerful than himself." One superhero origin story to get behind.
Lesser sooty owl	Still plenty sooty but doesn't get on your hands. But don't be touching owls.
Lestodon	Giant ground sloths are always depicted as prehistoric punching bags, but those claws probably dished out some major damage in their heyday.
Lichen	Wikipedia entry: "It is estimated that 6–8% of Earth's land surface is covered by lichens." Teamwork makes the dream work.
Lion	Less successful in colonizing the earth than lichen, but the team culture remains solid.
Madagascan flame tree	Also known as flame of the forest. Usually this is cause for alarm, but here it is cause for awe.
Madagascar tomato frog	 Very ripe. Do not squeeze.
Malus domestica	One cultivar's name: *Coeur de Boeuf*, or heart of beef. Might get confusing on a vegetarian menu.
Malus sieversii	Susceptible to fire blight, but who isn't?
Manatee	Not a sharp edge anywhere to be found on this round boy.
Mandarin duck	Restrained. Refined. Elegant. The stylings of the female mandarin duck get no respect.
Manta ray	Giant underwater social butterflies.
Margay	A tree ocelot, sized small.

Marginated tortoise	A shell skirt with a pretty plastron. Very matchy.
Marten	Loves German cars and chewing on warm ignition cables. Check your auto insurance policy to see what the marten deductible is. This is a real issue in Europe.
Mary River turtle	Sometimes rocks a green toupee made of algae. A bit obvious, but no judgment.
Meerkat	More a meer-mongoose.
Mexican burrowing toad	Oddball that branched off from other amphibians during the Jurassic. Who wouldn't get quirky being alone and underground for 190 million years?
Milky flesh (*Henneguya salminicola*)	Oddball that stopped using mitochondria or breathing oxygen a while back. Who wouldn't get a bit strange being alone and buried in salmon muscle tissue?
Mink	Always praised for what it provides instead of who it is. I see you, mink. I feel you.
Minke Whale	Producer of the West Pacific Biotwang, the funkiest of whale calls. It's always the shy ones that surprise you.
Minnow	Has value beyond being bait. A lake or stream without minnows is always sorrier for it.
Mola mola	

```
 |\
 Σ ‾‾‾\
 Σ  C ° 3
 Σ ___/
 |/
```

In ASCII art form, courtesy of the Monterey Bay Aquarium.

Mole cricket	Males shape their burrows into speakers to carry the mating songs they sing in pure tones. This is John Cusack *Say-Anything*-boombox-serenade level.
Monarch butterfly	The orange and black ones that are not tigers.

Monarch caterpillar	Picky eaters, like giant pandas. Yellow, black and white, like giant pandas asked to hold bananas.
Moorland hawker	Wikipedia entry: "Dragonfly nymphs can forcibly expel water in their rectum for rapid escape." Seems useful in a pinch.
Moose	Called an elk in Europe, which is a wapiti in North America and a completely different deer. Crystal clear.
Moray eel	Sports a second set of jaws inside its throat because sometimes one set isn't enough.
Mount Everest	Height can make up for a whole host of deficiencies, like being lacking in oxygen and being inhospitable.
Mountain beaver	Has bad kidneys that can't concentrate urine. What a weird finding to discover, which is now in your head.
Mudskipper	More floppers than prancers. Still, very impressive for a fish on land.
Muntjac deer	Also known as barking deer or rib-faced deer. Rib-face as a nickname? Not as good as T-bone.
Musk ox	Wikipedia entry: "Its Woods Cree names 'mâthi-môs' and 'mâthi-mostos' translate to 'ugly moose' and 'ugly bison,' respectively." Luckily, it is actually more like a glamour cow.
Musky rat-kangaroo	Completely different than a smelly kangaroo rat. Not even in the same ballpark.
Myanmar snub-nosed monkey	Do not play "got your nose" with it. It will not understand.
Naked mole rat	Tuber miners. Probably the most normal fact there is about them. Everything else is bananas, which they do not eat.
Narwhal	Unicorns, if they were to exist, should be called land narwhals.
Neon flying squid	Already has built-in jet propulsion. Flight seems like the logical next step.

Neutron star	Not a great vacation spot if you want to decompress.
North American least shrew	Never tell one to calm down or to chill. It will literally die.
North Chinese leopard	Provides leopard coverage in areas south of the Amur network, which is currently spotty at best.
Northern sea otter	Learns through touch. Likes to break down crabs and clams and sea urchins with its mitts. Would probably love a fidget spinner as a present.
Northern white rhinoceros	"You know, Fatu, we really are the last of us." If rhinos could talk.
Numbat	Can eat up to twenty thousand termites a day, a surprisingly calorie-friendly food.
Oak	Disappointing flowers, solid on everything else.
Ocellated icefish	No hemoglobin, no scales, no problem.
Ocelot	Not just a painted house cat, no matter what Salvador Dalí said of his pet ocelot, Babou.
Okapi	Not just a half-painted zebra or a pint-sized giraffe, but its own full Okapi self.
Opabinia	The multistalked eyes and clawed proboscis were probably bog standard for its time. Terribly out of fashion now.
Opah	Roundish. Do not break for celebration.
Ophthalmosaurus	Don't get into a staring contest with one. Even fossilized, those giant peepers seem like they can pierce your soul.
Ornate diamondback terrapin	Not quite turtle, not quite tortoise. Living in between at the salt marsh flats buffering land and sea.
Osprey	Piscivore, not pescatarian. Ordering for one at restaurants might get confusing.
Owl, a parliament of	Okay, this one is admittedly cool. Better than a wisdom, a hooting, or a stare.
Oyster	Tasty rocks.

Pacific anchovy	Tasty fish.
Pacific herring	Popular tasty fish, one size up.
Pacific salmon	Popular, tasty fish that likes to eat anchovies and herring. The circle of life is a big smorgasbord.
Pangolin	Can climb, can dig, can stink. So much more to them than their scales.
Parasitoid wasp	Can a parasitoid wasp parasitize another species of parasitoid wasp? I await answers on this *Inception*-level of madness.
Passenger pigeon	For those in the future able to travel back in time to watch their billion-strong flocks darken the skies, be sure to bring an umbrella.
Peanut worm	Sure, it looks like a peanut. Right.
Pen-tailed tree shrew	Drinks the equivalent of ten to twelve glasses of wine every night. That liver is putting in the work.
Peppered catfish	Does not actually come preseasoned.
Peppered moth	Also not seasoned, but birds can't taste spice anyway.
Peregrine falcon	Engages in speed-stooping. Look it up.
Persian carpet flatworm	Engages in penis fencing. Look it up. On second hand, maybe don't.
Peters's elephantnose fish	The nose is actually a chin. The name is also tricky to punctuate.
Pharaoh cuttlefish	Sometimes bends and waves its arms to imitate hermit crabs. Everything does eventually go crab it seems.
Philippine colugo	Comes accessorized with a furry snuggie for gliding and hiding.
Pikaia gracilens	On the verge of developing a head, which turned out to be an important feature for some. Sponges, on the other hand, never saw the point.
Piranha	"I've been known to reduce a piranha to a pile of bones in less than a minute." Jeremy Wade, host of Animal Planet's *River Monsters*, turning the tables.

Planarian flatworm	Resist the urge to draw a smile under the eyespots. Harder than it looks.
Pleasing fungus beetle	Resist the urge to release them into your home, even though they might add to the ambience.
Polar bear	Traditionally blubber-powered, but some Hudson Bay bears are hybrids these days, running on sea urchins, algae, and ducks.
Polyommatus **blue**	Do birds ever hesitate to snack on it, thinking it too dazzling to eat? Probably not.
Porbeagle	Not a dog, more a shark. Not a dogfish shark, more a mackerel shark. Not a mackerel.
Porcupine	Comes in crested and noncrested models. Barb availability on quills depends on region.
Porcupinefish	Decent sea urchin impersonator.
Portugese man o' war	Decent jellyfish impersonator.
Prairie lupine	Can fix nitrogen, can self-pollinate, can adjust their leaf hairs to reflect too much sun. Seems to have its act together.
Praya dubia	World's longest living Christmas light string.
Pronghorn	Not a goat or a deer or an antelope but its own thing. Should exchange contact information with the okapi to commiserate about being misunderstood.
Psittacosaurus	Beak and business in the front, wild with feather filaments in the back. A total party animal, in that it appeared to congregate in groups.
Puma	The quintessential all-American ranger, prowling from the Yukon to the Andes.
Pumpkin toadlet	Very small and very bad at jumping due to said smallness. It's an inner-ear balance thing.
Pumpkinseed fish	Bigger than a pumpkin seed. Much prettier too.
Puna flamingo	Could be a new yoga pose. Stand on one foot. Take in the wetland. Sift for brine shrimp. Take a nap. Hold.

Purple pincher hermit crab	Likes to climb, dig, and live in large groups called casts. More like purple pincher party crab.
Pygmy falcon	Weighs as much as a very small onion or fifty jelly beans. It's hard to find things that weigh two ounces for comparison.
Quaking aspen	Spans 108 acres or eighty-one football fields. It's hard to find things that get as big as a clonal colony for comparison.
Quokka	There are a lot of "only member of the genus _____" in Australia. This is another one of them.
Rabbit	Somewhat responsible for why there are so many "only member of the genus _____" in Australia. Thank you Victorian Acclimatization Society member Thomas Austin for unleashing them upon a continent.
Raccoon	Thank you to Redditor Carl Peligro for popularizing the nickname "trash panda." "Washbear" is a close second.
Rainbow trout	Upon listening to "Should I Stay or Should I Go" by The Clash, chose the former to remain in freshwater forever.
Rattlesnakes, a rhumba of	Sounds like the dance one does to get around the snakes.
Ravens, an unkindness of	An unfairness to, more like.
Red jungle fowl	Definitely came before the chicken.
Red panda	Not related to the giant version at all. *Panda* as a term isn't very useful, is it?
Red-billed quelea	Seednapper. "Africa's feathered locust." Males even sport a black mask.
Red-eared slider	Do not use in shuffleboard as shufflepuck.
Red-eyed tree frog	The go-to specimen for glamour shots. Use Australian green tree frogs for dopey pics.
Red-lipped batfish	The color is smudge-free, waterproof, and will never rub off.

Red-spotted coral crab	Provides guard duty for corals against sea stars and snails in exchange for room and food. Deserves a promotion in this day and age.
Reindeer	The deer variety, not the lichen variety, though the deer eats a lot of lichen, which eventually gets converted into deer.
Remora	Hitchhiking its way through life to wherever the whale/shark/turtle/dugong will bear it.
Rinderpest	Had a close to 100 percent fatality rate when untreated. Took the mass vaccination program seven years to eradicate.
RMS *Titanic*	Now home to a thriving bacterial community on the seafloor, where all can dine on first-class balustrades.
Roadrunner	Can fly. Which means it was just teasing the poor coyote this whole time.
Rock hyrax	Lives longer in colonies with more equal social ties. Fight the hierarchy.
Rock wallaby	Hopping and rock cliffs are usually not a natural fit, but here is another Australian exception, with seventeen species in the family embracing both every day.
Rocky mountain goat	Can develop a taste for human sweat and urine. Beware of pee-sniffing, salt-licking goats.
Roly-poly	A land crustacean. More a pill-shrimp than a pill-bug, conglobating all over your garden.
Rosy-faced lovebirds	Surprisingly accurate description of these little parrots. Wishing them all the happiness.
Rothschild giraffe	Taller than most giraffes, which is really saying something.
Round goby	Not that round.
Rufous hummingbird	Not that rufous. Maybe a bit on the face.
Saharan horned viper	Brow horns are made from modified scales. Maybe for glare protection, maybe for luring prey, but definitely a look. The original Blue Steel?

Saiga antelope	Does not drink through its trunk nose, but water will probably come out if it hears a funny joke while drinking. This has not been officially tested.
Sailfish	Sporting the most badass of hairdos—the foldable mohawk/mullet combo.
San Francisco garter snake	Gorgeous. Gets a bit stinky when stressed, but who doesn't?
Saurosuchus	Not exactly a lizard as the name suggests and not exactly a crocodile. Probably not the first thing to come to mind if being chased by this twenty-five-foot-long apex predator.
Saury	Festivals are held in its name in Japan every year, but mostly on celebrating ways to eat it. Celebrity culture, a mixed bag.
Scale-eye plaice	Flatfish that was formerly round. Simply seeking a stretch of sand to settle soundly. Sorry (not saury).
Scorpionfish	A hazard on par with the invertebrate and the pepper iterations. Don't tread on one.
Screaming hairy armadillo	Not to be confused with the pink fairy armadillo. A sample of its call makes for a good alarm sound.
Sculpin	A fish that's a fifty-fifty mix of soft to spiny, and a seventy-thirty mix of head to body.
Sea cucumber	Can form herds that roam across the seafloor, unlike land sea cucumbers, which stay put.
Sea vase	Also called a vase tunicate. Not great for holding flowers for reasons that are not entirely its fault.
Seahorse	Places near last in any swimming race. Prefers to hang out in the rear with the porcupinefish.
Sendai crow	Official cliques include stone crows, which put rocks on railway tracks; fire crows, which steal candles from shrines; soap crows, which go into bathrooms and eat soap; and faucet crows, which have learned to turn on taps. A fun bunch.
Sengi	Reigning speed champ in the petite mammals (under a kilogram) division.

Serama bantam (chicken)	A very small chicken. A big shot among quails.
Sergeant major damselfish	Its rank is not officially recognized by any military at this time.
Serval	The spots and stripes on its coat look like they could be converted to dots and dashes. Secret agent cat?
Sessile oak	Really doesn't like to move, even compared to other oaks.
Seven-armed octopus	Blobbier than a standard octopus. The eighth arm is tucked under the right eye and is used to deliver sperm. The previous sentence exists and is true.
Shasta crayfish	Makes itself scarce in the presence of louder, bigger signal crayfish.
Shasta salamander	Makes itself scarce in the presence of dam construction and limestone quarrying.
Shastasaurus	Whale-sized and toothless; possibly a suction feeder. Squid slurping seems to be a universal pastime for big swimming things.
Shepherd tree	A different way to shepherd: Instead of running after things, attract them to you.
Shiny cowbird	Females are more matte tan than shiny black. Makes it easier for them to smuggle their eggs into other bird's nests. Those sneaky brood parasites.
Shire horse	Must look even more giant to hobbits, who are so used to ponies.
Short-faced bear	Face seems fine, just deeper set, which makes it look more like a soul bear.
Shortfin mako shark	Very sharp. Pointy bits every which way.
Silkworm	Firm and unwavering believer that mulberry leaf is the one and perfect food.
Silver sprat	Firm and unwavering believer that zooplankton is the one and perfect food.

Silver-backed chevrotain	Will eat any green, leafy, grassy thing within reach, along with fallen fruit and the occasional bug. More chill about the food thing.
Silverside	Fish. Very small, very shiny, and hard to count.
Singing scallop	More of a branding name for this West coast mollusk. Musical genes don't seem to run in the phylum.
Skate	A less bony, more symmetrical flatfish. Good glider like the footwear but works underwater instead of above it.
Skipjack tuna	Muscle packed into the shape of a football. Fit and geared for swimming so it can hunt so it can eat so it can swim some more.
Slender sea pen	Does not write well at all. Floppy to hold and the ink bleeds everywhere.
Sloth bear	All bears are sloth bears at times, but a sloth bear might be the slothiest.
Smallpox	Not welcomed back to this world ever, thank you very much.
Snake blenny	Multipurpose moniker. To qualify as one, simply be small, longish but not too eel-ish, and hang out near the sea bottom.
Snares penguin	Breeds only on the Snares, islands that are covered with tree daisies. More forest-based than ice-based.
Snow leopard	Uses its tail for fat storage and a face blanket. Which sound like the best uses for a tail.
Sociable weaver bird	Somewhere there must be an introvert weaver bird, just wanting some alone time in its chamber.
Sockeye salmon	Means so much to so many. Bears, people, forests, and rivers—they all harbor traces of this fish.
Somali ostrich	A big bird that's as tall as Big Bird. Can't write poetry or roller-skate though.
Southern dart (moth)	Faster than your average throwing dart. Hard to aim.

Southern elephant seal	Spends its alone time at sea before getting rowdy in groups on land. Maintains a good work-life balance.
Southern flannel moth	Wikipedia entry for the caterpillar's venomous spines: "Victims describe the pain as similar to a broken bone or blunt-force trauma." This real-life tribble that packs a punch.
Southern fulmar	Derived from Old Norse as "foul-mew" or "foul-gull" due to seabirds spitting foul-smelling oil at hunters taking their eggs. On the side of the birds here, really.
Southern fur seal	Opted for the half-fur, half-blubber option for insulation instead of going full fat.
Southern hairy-nosed wombat	Just needs a trimmer and a move to the equator to start a new life simply as "wombat."
Southern sea otter	Not that far south, really, just down to California.
Southern tamandua	Some sport a black fur vest, while others come in blond coats. Seems to dress for the region instead of for the occasion.
Sparrowhawk	Best wizard. Decent bird.
Sperm whale	Has pruney skin. Can't unwrinkle if you don't get out of the water.
Sphinx moth	Some can hover, fly backward, refuel on the wing. Blurring the line between insect and hummingbird.
Spotted hyena	Actually laughs when stressed and giggles after being attacked. No joke.
Spotted rose snapper	A big ol' black spot smack-dab on its side of beautiful scales. A source of confusion for both predators and admirers.
Spring peeper	How can something the size of a paper clip be so loud?
Springbok	The deluxe, speedier model of a Thomson's gazelle. Sports great shocks.

Springhare	A rodent that's named for a rabbit that hops like a kangaroo. Also glows orange and pink under UV light.
Star-nosed mole	It being able to smell underwater by blowing bubbles is arguably the least interesting thing about it.
Starburst anemone	Formerly thought to be a separated form of the aggregating anemone but is now considered divorced from it and is its own entity.
Star pearlfish	Up to fifteen fish can squat inside one sea cucumber anus. The housing market's rough out there.
Strawberry anemone	Will sting other anemones encroaching on its turf. Strawberries on land seem more relaxed about sharing their patch.
Sumatran rhinoceros	The reddish fuzzy one that likes to roll around in the mud.
Sundew	The dewy glistening one that likes to lurk inside the bog.
Suraka silk moth	The caterpillars can spin wild silks. The adults can impersonate owls. A very creative family.
Sweetgum tree	Don't chew on the bark.
Swordfish	More of a slasher than a piercer. Definitely more of a fighter than a lover.
***Takhi* (horse)**	Sports a dun coat with pangaré features and primitive markings—the latest fall collection from Przewalski's.
Tarantula	On an all-liquid diet of centipede juice, mouse juice, or bat juice—the type depends on the species.
Teddy bear crab	Covered in setae. Think the wet fur of a childhood stuffy that hasn't been washed for decades.
Tenrec	Arrived on Madagascar by raft. Stayed to build lives as climbers, burrowers, and fishers. A classic immigrant success story.

Thalassocnus	Sloths that tried their hand at sea living like seals and iguanas, but things didn't work out. The dugong competition for eelgrass might have been too fierce.
Thick-billed murre	Northern hemisphere's closest version of penguins now that the great auk is gone. Decent counterfeit if you don't look too close, or up at the sky.
Three-toed sloth	Mostly diurnal while the two-toed sloth is nocturnal. Beware trees, your leaves are in danger twenty-four seven!
Tiktaalik	Miss it? Visit your local gar for a rough reminder of what one looks like.
Tinamou	Homebodies. A bit shy, a bit drab, reluctant to get out of their comfort zone. Prowling jaguars might be a hidden source of trauma.
Tongue-eating louse	Out of a job and a home if the fish dies. Not many openings for replacement tongues out there.
Topi	To-pi Ante-Lope. Getting a bit loopy after writing four-hundred-plus of these.
Toxoplasmosis gondii	Has a thing for felines. Steer your cats clear of this parasite.
Triceratops	Can't seem to shake free of those tyrannosaur associations even after sixty-five million years.
Trilobite	Extinct but not forgotten, because their fossils show up everywhere and won't let anyone forget.
Trinidad Moruga scorpion (pepper)	Do not eat unless you are a masochist or a bird, which does not have receptors for capsaicin, in which case, go to town!
Tropical flying fish	Comes in two-winged models for speed and four-winged models for lift.
Tuatara	A lizard-like nonlizard with a third eye and no eardrums. Chilling with the other oddities on Te Ika-a-Māui in Aotearoa.

Tufted capuchin	Understands how to clean up spills with paper towels, which is more than can be said for many a teenager.
Tumbleweed	A kindred companion to the Dude as he meanders through life, drinking half-and-half at the supermarket. Always adrift, always abides.
Turkey vulture	Follows its nose, unlike toucans. Tough to have a vulture mascot on a box of cereal though.
Two-toed sloth	Is it really upside down if it spends most of its life that way? Right side up depends on one's perspective.
Ugrunaaluk kuukpikensis	Lived high up in the Arctic Circle. Imagine herds of thirty-foot-long reptilian reindeer.
Velvet pitcher plant	Imagine trying to learn everything about a species from a single specimen. Akin to summarizing humanity via Gary from next door.
Venus flower basket	Actually a glass sponge. Yes, those are things and there are reefs of them. Remember, oceans.
Vinegar mother	Basically a party-island bacteria fashioned out of cellulose to keep partying while converting alcohol into vinegar.
Virginia possum	Surprisingly short-lived with a life expectancy of around two years. Live Hard. Die fast. Eat everything.
Visagie's golden mole	So secretive that it could only be found once.
Walrus	One of the rare animals that skips the baby phase entirely. Born fully whiskered.
Wapiti	Chunky and surprisingly noisy. Can occasionally be majestic.
Warthog	Enjoys an occasional tick removal session from banded mongooses. Not from meerkats, unfortunately.
Water anole	One-ups *Indohyus* when it comes to diving to escape predators by bringing its own rebreather.

Waterbuck	"A robust build." "Rather sedentary in nature." "Exudes a turpentine odor that is disliked by predators." Kudos to the waterbuck in subverting conventional antelope expectations.
Wattled jacana	Daily dad duties include picking chicks up from caiman-infested waters and walking them over to caiman-free lily pads.
Waving glass frog	As fragile as advertised. Handle delicately, preferably not at all.
Weddell seal	Dinner sausage of choice for at least one pod of pack ice orcas.
West African lungfish	Dinner sausage of choice for many a shoebill stork.
White clover	Odds for a four-leaf clover are 1 in 5,076, according to a Swiss survey of 5.7 million clovers. Researchers might need to take a break afterward.
Whitemargin unicornfish	Don't stare. It's not polite.
White-nest swiftlet	Everyone wants the art, not the artist.
White-spotted pufferfish	Was named "Top Ten New Species" discovered in 2014 by the International Institute for Species Exploration but was too busy building nests to claim its prize.
White-tailed deer	Real-life Bambi, just with more ticks and nasal botflies.
Wild boar	Tough pig. Might gore.
Wild ibex (Himalayan)	Tough goat. Nice horns.
Wild mustard	A green, an oil, a condiment. The original superfood.
Wildebeest	Gets along famously with zebras, which is no small feat.
William's dwarf gecko	Too showy for its own good. The pet trade loves electric blue, whether it be on crayfish or lizards.

Wolf	Alpha wolves do not exist. Lone wolves yearn to start a new family. Best to drop the dated myths on this most social and cooperative of canines.
Wolverine	Definitely a loner. Scared of wolves. Known also as skunk bear or nasty cat.
Wombat	Furry loaf from Australia. Comes in small and medium sizes. Poops out cubes.
Yellow dent corn	The corn in high-fructose corn syrup. Not for direct eating but for indirect mass consumption.
Yellow-rumped leaf-eared mouse	Amidst the rock and ice of a twenty-two-thousand-foot-tall volcano lies a fortress of solitude for one mighty mouse.
Yellow underwing moth	Goes through a destructive adolescent phase by cutting down stems of all the plants in its vicinity. Calms down after getting its wings.
Yellow-belly slider	Sometimes mates with red-eared sliders. Does not make an orange cross, unfortunately.
Yeti crab	Has more confirmed sightings than the Loch Ness monster, the chupacabra, and the Mothman put together.
Yucatan mini-pig	Not so mini, weighing as much as a person. Scary snorer.
Zebra	How to design for visual accessibility: the classic example.
Zebra shark	Young sharks sport stripes while adults sport spots. Hard to change the name at this point, with leopard sharks, jaguar sharks, and pajama sharks all spoken for.

Acknowledgments

I'm grateful to the following publications in which essays from this book first appeared, sometimes in earlier forms: *AGNI*, "Utter, Earth"; *Gulf Coast Online*, "Second Best is Best"; *Pleiades*, "A Hearth is a Kind of Home"; *Present Tense*, "Going Down to Ground," formerly known as "Nine-Tenths"; the Center for Humans and Nature, "The Perfect Party Guest," formerly known as "Picking the Perfect Party Guest" and "Giving Up on Your Dreams"; *The Hopper*, "Life Lessons of the Odd and Ancient"; *The Willowherb Review*, "Yes, You Can Leave the Hospital Without Naming Your Baby"; and *Wildness*, "A School is a Type of Shoal."

Thank you to *AGNI* editors Bill Pierce and Jennifer Alise Drew for helping shape the essay that would become the title and backbone of this collection. Thank you to David Naimon for nominating it for inclusion in the 2023 Pushcart Prize anthology.

Thank you to the Jan Michalski Foundation for Literature for affording me the space to begin this project, and to the Hanse-Wissenschaftskolleg (HWK) Institute of Advanced Studies for providing me with the time to complete it. Thank you to the Berlin *Akademie der Künste* and the NEUSTART CULTUR program for the funding support. I'm forever grateful to the Beaty Biodiversity Museum for opening my eyes to so many of the odd and wonderful creatures that once and still abound on this earth.

Thank you to the organizers of the Bread Loaf Environmental Conference and the Orion Omega Environmental Conference for providing me with the opportunity to connect with the nature-writing community. I am indebted to my teachers there, Craig Childs and Megan Mayhew Bergman, respectively, for their insights and their votes of confidence to keep writing.

Thank you to my agent, Akin Akinwumi, and small press champion Derek Krissoff for believing in this oddball project from the outset. Thanks to my friends from the Simon Fraser University Southbank creative writing program for providing accountability and solidarity over the years. Thank you, Mom and Jack, for your unconditional support in all my creative endeavors.

Thank you to Michaela Vieser, my partner in life and literature, for being my sounding board, my first reader, my biggest fan.